P9-AFC-495

REVOLT
IN THE BOARDROOM

Also by ALAN MURRAY

Nonfiction

> *The Wealth of Choices: How the New Economy Puts Power in Your Hands and Money in Your Pockets*
>
> *Showdown at Gucci Gulch: Lawmakers, Lobbyists and the Unlikely Triumph of Tax Reform (with Jeffrey Birnbaum)*

UNM-GALLUP   DUP

3 7996 1006 7732 3

REVOLT
IN THE BOARDROOM

*The New Rules of Power
in Corporate America*

ALAN
MURRAY

Collins
An Imprint of HarperCollinsPublishers

REVOLT IN THE BOARDROOM. Copyright © 2007 by Alan Murray. All rights reserved. Printed in the United States of America. No part of this book may be used or reproduced in any manner whatsoever without written permission except in the case of brief quotations embodied in critical articles and reviews. For information, address HarperCollins Publishers, 10 East 53rd Street, New York, NY 10022.

HarperCollins books may be purchased for educational, business, or sales promotional use. For information, please write: Special Markets Department, HarperCollins Publishers, 10 East 53rd Street, New York, NY 10022.

FIRST EDITION

Designed by Jaime Putorti

Library of Congress Cataloging-in-Publication Data

Murray, Alan S., 1954–
    Revolt in the boardroom : the new rules of power in corporate America / Alan Murray.
        p.   cm.
    1. Corporate governance—United States.   2. Boards of directors— United States.   3. Chief executive officers—United States.   4. Power (Social sciences)—United States.   5. Corporations—Social aspects—United States.   I. Title.

HD2785.M87   2007
658.4'22—dc22   2006051898

ISBN: 978-0-06-088247-1

07   08   09   10   11   DIX/RRD   10 9 8 7 6 5 4 3 2 1

To Lori,
who made this book,
and so much else that's worthwhile in my life, possible

CONTENTS

INTRODUCTION

In November of 2004, Paul Steiger, the managing editor of the *Wall Street Journal*, asked me to start a new column that he wanted to call, simply, "Business."

It was an unusual request. I had spent my career with the *Wall Street Journal* in Washington, D.C., writing about the intersection of politics and business, but from the political side of that intersection. For nearly a decade, I had run the paper's Washington bureau, and for three years, I had run the Washington bureau of CNBC television. Just two months earlier, I had been tied to an anchor desk broadcasting hourly updates on the twists and turns of the final days of the presidential campaign. And now I was supposed to write a column called "Business"?

During my two decades working for Paul, however, I had learned to appreciate his wisdom and trust his judgment. I left Washington behind and moved with my family—against some protest—to Connecticut to begin a new journey, not sure where it would lead.

It didn't take long to find out.

The first "Business" column, which ran on February 2, 2005, was about Carly Fiorina, the Hewlett-Packard CEO whose struggles with her board of directors had been exposed in an unusual front-page piece by my colleague Pui-Wing Tam—the story that later sparked a controversial investigation into boardroom leaks. I followed Fiorina to the annual Davos schmooze-fest in Switzerland—the last place she should have been at the time, given her problems—and confronted her with a question about her relationship with the Hewlett-Packard board. Her terse response, delivered with the fire of anger in her eyes, was "Excellent."

Less than two weeks later, she was fired.

Fiorina's firing was quickly followed by that of Harry Stonecipher, chief executive of Boeing, who had an affair with another executive—hardly uncommon among CEOs in the past—and then had the astonishingly bad judgment to write about it in a series of graphic e-mails. Then came Hank Greenberg—the prototype of the "imperial CEO"—who was forced out of the top job at American International Group that he had held for three decades. A few months later, Philip Purcell was dumped as the top man at Morgan Stanley.

As I watched from my columnist's perch, CEOs fell like bowling pins. Michael Eisner had left Disney just a few months earlier, and Franklin Raines had been ousted as CEO of Fannie Mae. Raymond Gilmartin at Merck, Hank McKinnell at Pfizer and Peter Dolan at Bristol-Myers Squibb toppled in the months soon after, followed by William McGuire at UnitedHealth Group. The specifics of each case were different. But the result was the same: a powerful CEO tossed out of a job against his or her will by forces too strong to resist.

This was something new in American corporate life. During the 1960s, '70s and '80s, the public firing of a big-company CEO was virtually unknown. Starting in the 1990s, a few boards had the gumption to oust the top man at poorly performing companies—GM, IBM, American Express—but the instances were still relatively few and far between. For the most part, chief executives of big American companies continued to stride the world stage like giants. At a time when democracy was spreading and hierarchies everywhere were crumbling, CEOs continued to hold surprising unilateral power. Men like Bill Gates of Microsoft, Jack Welch of General Electric, Sandy Weill of Citigroup, wielded largely unquestioned authority over their sprawling organizations, traversing the planet in private jets, determining the fates of hundreds of thousands of employees, and enjoying levels of pay and benefits that enabled them to live like royalty . . . or better.

Those icons left the scene, however, as the new century witnessed a string of calamitous events—the collapse of the stock market bubble, the terror attacks of September 11 and the corporate scandals of Enron, WorldCom, Adelphia, Tyco. Suddenly, the public perception of CEOs plummeted. Regulators, legislators and attorneys general swung into action. New laws and new listing requirements for public companies were rushed into place. Giant pension funds and their reformist allies began to flex their muscles more, looking to exert more control over corporations. Within a remarkably short period of time, the corporate world was transformed.

The most visible manifestation of that transformation was the spate of CEO firings that began with Disney's Michael Eisner in 2004 and has continued right up until the publication of this book. Corporate beheadings have become endemic. According to the executive recruiting firm Challenger, Gray & Christmas, U.S. firms were on track to fire or lose a record 1,400 CEOs in 2006, up from 1,322 in 2005, and nearly double the 663 in 2004. The tenure of CEOs was getting shorter each year.

Something new was afoot in corporate America. The roots of change could be found in the democratization of stock ownership, the rise of the great pension funds, the flowering of "nongovernmental organizations" and in the shareholder rights battles, takeover fights and corporate governance reforms of earlier decades. In the new century, following the market's collapse and the spate of corporate scandals, the trend became a revolution.

By the time I started the "Business" column in February of 2005, that revolution was well under way. The ancient regime was gone. The corporation, which had been the very foundation of 20th-century prosperity, was in metamorphosis. A new order was waiting to be born.

■

Before the new order emerged, however, there would be disorder. The CEO firings signaled widespread rejection of an old way of doing business. No one quite knew yet, however, what the new way would be. In boardrooms across the country, directors struggled to understand the changed rules of corporate power. Their struggles often resulted in confusion rather than clarity.

Once again, Hewlett-Packard provided the clearest window into the turmoil.

Carly Fiorina had been ousted from her job in February 2005 because she acted too much like a CEO of the old world. She expected to rule her domain with unquestioned authority.

Her board of directors, meanwhile, was struggling to come to grips with the new world. It was a world in which the directors could no longer sit back and simply let the CEO hold sway. In the new world, they were held to account by shareholders, regulators, and even the public at large for the company's performance. As directors at Enron and WorldCom had found, directors could even be forced to pay large sums of money out of their own pockets for the company's misdeeds.

In short, boards of directors, once a clubby gathering of the CEO's friends and advisers, now suddenly mattered. As the CEO's power had waned, the board's power had grown—buoyed by the requirements of new laws and new stock exchange listing requirements, and by the demands of shareholders and regulators and a host of others who wanted CEOs to be held in check. How to exercise that new power became a matter of hot debate.

Nowhere was that debate hotter than inside the Hewlett-Packard boardroom in the months following Fiorina's departure. The dull-sounding subject of "corporate governance" became the cause for sharp-elbowed boardroom battles, with warring egos offering competing visions of how the company should be run.

On one side of that battle was the company's nonexecutive chairman Patricia Dunn, who, while struggling with cancer, was also trying to turn HP into a model of post-Enron probity. She was a stickler for proper rules and procedures, and her strong sense of propriety compelled her to investigate the boardroom leaks that had plagued Fiorina's final days.

On the other side of the battle was a swashbuckling venture capitalist, Tom Perkins, who had sat on the boards of dozens of smaller companies, where the huge sums he had invested gave him equally huge sway. Perkins had little tolerance for the new requirements of boardroom etiquette, or for Dunn's procedural niceties. He would erupt in rage when they got in his way. At times, he would poke Dunn in the clavicle and shout, "I made you chairman."

For a year and a half, that debate raged in the privacy of the HP boardroom. Then in September of 2006, it broke into public view when I published the first account of the HP board's showdown in an unusual installment of the "Business" column, which started on the front page of the *Journal*. The story told how Dunn's leak investigation had turned into an out-of-control spying venture, pinpointing the leaker but also triggering investigations by state and government officials. Perkins, angry with Dunn for airing the investigation with the full board and exposing his friend George "Jay" Keyworth as a leaker, quit the board in a huff, and later alerted legal authorities. Prodded by Perkins, the California attorney general charged Dunn and others at the company with fraud in conducting the investigation.

To most analysts, this Hewlett-Packard fiasco was seen as sui generis—a unique and unusually potent combination of circumstances and people. It was more than that. It was the most visible manifestation of a revolution that was happening to some degree at every big company in the country. For better or worse, it was the chaos of a new order emerging.

I had left Washington after more than two decades of writing about the power struggles that defined that capital city only to find myself, once again, writing about a monumental battle for power.

My new beat, it turned out, was not all that different from my old one.

In March of 2006, I was invited to speak to the Business Council, a group of chief executives of the largest companies in the United States. The meeting took place at the Boca Raton Resort and Club, one of south Florida's oldest and most luxurious resorts. As was their custom, the CEOs arrived mostly in corporate jets, met for dinner and morning discussion sessions, then devoted the afternoon to golf.

The Business Council had been formed back in the Roosevelt administration, and often used its morning sessions for meetings with government officials, to talk about matters of public policy. Usually, the confident executives who attended were less interested in receiving knowledge than imparting it.

This meeting, however, had a different topic—a topic that the CEOs couldn't fully comprehend, that made many of them anxious. The topic: corporate reputations. Or to be more precise, *their* reputations.

It had been almost five years since the Enron scandal exploded, yet CEOs were still feeling the aftershocks. Instead of subsiding, those aftershocks seemed to be growing in intensity. The image of the CEO remained stubbornly low in the public's mind. As a result, the world of the CEO was changing—rapidly, dramatically, and to them, inexplicably.

They wanted to hear from journalists and political pollsters just why they were held in such low esteem by the public and the press. They were like struggling politicians battling disturbingly low approval ratings. They had come to realize—or at least some of them had come to realize—that public corporations needed the approval of a broader public in order to succeed.

I had first attended a meeting of the Business Council back in 1984, when I was a new reporter in the Washington bureau of the *Wall Street Journal* and was sent by my bureau chief, Albert Hunt, to interview some of the CEOs in attendance. At the time, the group met at The Homestead, a grand and historic resort built next to hot mineral springs in the mountains of western Virginia that had been entertaining guests since 1766. Both Thomas Jefferson and James Madison are said to have visited the resort. Financier J. Pierpont Morgan was a regular, and a major investor.

While the CEOs came by private jet to the tiny Warm Springs airport nearby, I took the 210-mile mountainous trip from Washington by car, a much more arduous journey. Checking into my room, however, I found a bottle of aged Scotch whiskey waiting for me, along with a box of quality cigars and a three-foot-tall basket of fruit. A card attached said: "To A. Murray. Compliments of The Homestead."

Not bad duty, I thought. It wasn't until the next day that I realized the then–chief executive of Mobil Oil Corporation was named Allen E. Murray and that he was attending the meeting. There was a very good possibility the Scotch, cigars and fruit were all meant for him, not me.

Embarrassed, I tracked down Murray and explained what had happened. "No problem," he said. "But do you know some guy named Al Hunt? He's calling every ten minutes demanding to talk to me, and I told the front desk I've never heard of the guy."

In 2001, I was invited to another Business Council meeting, this time at the Greenbrier Resort in West Virginia, which had a pedigree as long as The Homestead's, and housed a bomb shelter built for the entire U.S. Congress in case of a nuclear strike. The topic of this meeting was energy, and I was asked to moderate a panel that included a number of experts, but most notably Kenneth Lay, the CEO of the Enron Corporation.

At the time, Lay attracted admiration and envy from most of his CEO colleagues. His company was seen as one of the most innovative in the country, having shed its image as a stodgy gas pipeline company and developed new markets in not just natural gas and electricity, but everything from weather futures to broadband Internet services. He was widely respected as a forward-thinking expert on energy matters, and had advised the newly elected Bush administration on its policy plans. His chief executive colleagues listened to his words with intense interest, treating him with the utmost respect.

It was only a few months later that Enron's house of cards collapsed, after questions were raised about private partnerships that had been created to get some of the company's assets off the books. That turned out to be the leading edge of a wave of scandal that sparked outrage and led to extensive corporate and regulatory changes. And no one felt the ramifications of those changes more profoundly than the 100 or so executives of big public companies who made up the membership of the Business Council.

For a while, many of the CEOs thought the scandal would blow over. Several told me they were appalled at the next meeting of the group, when Lay showed up. He was an embarrassment to them; they wanted nothing more to do with him.

As time passed, however, it became increasingly clear that the corporate scandals would not blow over. There had been a sea change in regulation and law enforcement, in the behavior of shareholders, and in the organizational structure of the corporation. Most important, and underpinning it all, was a sea change in public attitudes.

That's why, in the spring of 2006, the topic on these CEOs' minds was reputation. They were still trying to come to grips with how their world had changed so thoroughly in such a short time. Some of them blamed the press. They felt that excessive journalistic focus on accounting scandals and high CEO pay gave the public a misimpression of large corporations. Others seemed to recognize that the press's focus on these issues reflected broader social forces as much as it influenced those forces. There was a public revolt under way, and CEOs were the targets.

Many of these men and women had no doubt spent much of their lives dreaming of becoming a CEO. For a businessperson, it was a pinnacle of achievement. The post, they thought, would allow them to command vast resources and enjoy widespread respect.

By 2006, however, the job had changed. To the outside world, the CEO might still have seemed to possess unparalleled authority. Most still were garnering oversized paychecks. But to those who actually held the post, it was clear that much of the power had drained away.

For one thing, as Carly Fiorina learned, CEOs had to take their boards of directors much more seriously. Boards were becoming increasingly independent, with members chosen by board committees rather than by the CEO. Usually, the executive still had a say and could veto a new board member that seemed particularly troublesome. But boards were no longer handpicked.

For another, independent board members now met regularly in executive session, without managers present—a profound change for the CEO. That gave members much more of an opportunity to talk freely about their misgivings concerning the CEO and the management team—something that they were much less likely to do when the CEO was sitting in the room.

Under New York Stock Exchange listing requirements enacted after the scandals, boards were also urged to have a "lead" or "presiding" director—someone who provided information to the board, and organized its sessions. CEOs had in the past been able to keep boards under their control, in part, by chairing the sessions, setting the agenda, and filtering information. Now, someone else had that role. In a few companies, like Hewlett-Packard after Ms. Fiorina left, lead independent directors had even taken on the title of "chairman of the board."

Boards also had far more responsibility than they had had in the past. Increasingly, the accountants and the compensation consultants reported to the board, not the CEO. That meant directors had to spend far more time digging deep into the affairs of the company. Several board members told me that the average amount of time they spent on board affairs more than quadrupled in the post-Enron world.

Underlying all of that was the very real fear of board members that if they weren't careful, they could be held personally accountable for the actions of the corporations. That's what had happened to directors at Enron and WorldCom, and other directors understood that it could happen to them, as well.

The changes in the corporate world went far beyond the boardroom. Large institutional shareholders were increasingly flexing their muscles. CEOs could still count on the big mutual fund companies that were their largest shareholders—Fidelity Investments, Barclays Global Investors, Vanguard Group—to support them most of the time, in part because those companies were also interested in winning the corporation's business.

But other investors were becoming increasingly feisty. Big public-employee pension funds, like CalPERS, were weighing in on an ever-wider range of issues, such as the selection of directors and CEO pay. Sometimes they teamed up with nongovernmental organizations like the Rainforest Action Network or the Interfaith Center on Corporate Responsibility, which had entirely different agendas: preventing deforestation in developing countries, stopping the spread of HIV/AIDS in Africa, or promoting a "living wage."

Then there were the hedge funds. They were relatively new to the corporate scene, but had built up assets in excess of a trillion dollars. And their real clout came from their willingness to move quickly. If they saw an opportunity to oust a troubled CEO—like Phil Purcell at Morgan Stanley, for instance—they would quickly buy up stock and become major shareholders, agitating for change.

Regulators also had new resources and a new resolve to police the corporate world. So did state officials like Eliot Spitzer, the feisty attorney general of New York. By the middle of 2006, Spitzer was focused on a new goal: becoming governor of New York. But he had blazed a trail that was sure to be followed by other ambitious attorneys general—many of whom seemed to believe that "AG" stood for "aspiring governor." In September of 2006, for instance, the California attorney general, Bill Lockyer, took a page straight from the Spitzer playbook in his very public investigation of whether Hewlett-Packard had used improper methods in investigating boardroom leaks.

Underlying all of this was the continued public disapproval of large corporations. In a Gallup poll taken in November 2005, just 16 percent of Americans said they thought highly of business executives, down 10 points in five years. For companies that relied on their reputations to do business—companies like General Electric, Wal-Mart, or Procter & Gamble—lack of public support was a very big problem indeed.

For CEOs, all of this meant that their tenure was likely to be shorter and more uncertain, and their job was certain to be tougher than it had been for their predecessors. The immense power and influence that had characterized the American CEO in the last half of the 20th century was clearly on the wane. Meanwhile, other groups that wanted a say in the running of big corporations were fighting to fill the vacuum.

Suddenly, America's great wealth-generating machine—the 20th-century public corporation—didn't seem so great anymore.

■

The thesis of this book is this: Public corporations, which were the most successful institutional creation of the 20th century, are in the midst of radical change. That change has far greater and more wide-ranging implications than most commentators recognize or are willing to admit. The media still portrays the chief executive officer as the center of the corporate universe. In fact, the CEO has been greatly diminished, and now shares power with an array of others—boards of directors, regulators, pension fund managers, hedge fund managers, accountants, lawyers, nongovernmental organizations—all of whom are eager to have their say in the corporation's affairs. The strongest evidence for this thesis is found in the remarkable string of CEO firings that began in late 2004 and continued through 2006.

As this book will demonstrate, the forces driving that change show no sign of abating. Outrage over excessive CEO pay, in particular, seems certain to fuel the revolution for some time to come. The 20th-century economy saw the pinnacle of the CEO-centric global corporation. The 21st century is watching something very different emerge.

From its beginnings, the primary goal of the corporation has been to make money. But this 21st-century revolution is about more than money. It is about power. Large corporations have come to dominate economic life. As a result, they attract power-seekers of all stripes—from nakedly ambitious politicians like Eliot Spitzer to wily idealists like Michael Brune of the Rainforest Action Network, all of whom have found in the weakened state of business an opportunity.

Big business has become big politics. The very success of corporations in the 20th century has made them the top targets of the 21st. As a result, the men and women who run big companies are forced to act more like politicians, responding to an ever-growing set of demands. Concern for "shareholders" has been replaced by a broad appeal to "stakeholders"—a vague notion that takes in untold numbers of people and issues. When I asked A. G. Lafley, the chief executive of Procter & Gamble, to tell me who his "stakeholders" were, he started talking about his shareholders, his employees, his customers, his consumers, and the communities in which all these people lived. Before long, he had included, by my rough calculation, half the people on the planet. Chief executives like Lafley, hammered by a cynical public, had come to realize that, at the end of the day, the companies they ran were dependent on broad public support for their survival.

This book is an early effort to describe the transformation of the corporation, and the battle for corporate power, that is now under way in the United States and to some extent across the globe. Like all such journalistic efforts, it suffers from a lack of distance. The trend is undeniable, but its ultimate resolution remains unclear. The old corporation was one of the singular successes of the 20th century, creating vast amounts of wealth and prosperity around the globe. The new corporation will be something different. But what?

Optimists see a more responsive, more democratic, more socially responsible institution emerging from the upheaval. Pessimists fear that the very same ills that plague modern-day politics—polarization, divisiveness, and stalemate—may come to hobble corporations.

Much is at stake. Just as the corporation defined economic progress in the last century, its fate will set the course of the current century. The dramatic power struggles that now are playing out in the CEO suite and the boardroom will, in the end, determine what kinds of lives and what kind of world our children and our children's children inherit.

CHAPTER ONE

REVOLT IN
THE BOARDROOM

1 ||||||||||||||||||||||||||||||||||

On Monday, January 10, 2005, Carly Fiorina sat at the very pinnacle of corporate power.

Since 1999, she had been chairman and chief executive of one of the world's most storied technology companies, Hewlett-Packard, which employed 150,000 people and brought in revenues exceeding $80 billion a year—roughly the economic output of Nigeria. She had doubled those revenues by engineering a controversial merger with Compaq Computer Corporation in 2002—a merger that had been contested publicly by Walter Hewlett, son of one of the company's revered founders. It had been a grueling, vicious and highly personal battle for her.

But she had won.

In the process, Carly Fiorina had proven herself to be one of the most talented business leaders of her generation. She was charismatic and compelling—able to win the hearts and minds of audiences large or small. As one executive who worked with her at Lucent Technologies Inc. put it, "She could sell ice to Eskimos." Because of that skill, she was now widely heralded as the most powerful woman in business. She traveled the world, giving hundreds of public speeches, and frequently graced the covers of business magazines. She made such an impression on the public consciousness that, in many business circles, she could be easily identified by one name alone.

She was Carly.

Her position and her power—like those of her colleagues at the very top of the corporate pyramid—in some ways rivaled the position and power of great rulers. At the turn of the century, CEOs were unconstrained by powerful ministers or legislators, unchallenged in meaningful elections, unencumbered by burdensome constitutional constraints, and usually unthreatened by rebellious underlings. The previous century had seen the flattening of political hierarchies throughout the world. But at the giant corporations that spanned the globe, controlled much of the world's commerce and generated much of the world's wealth, the CEO still sat on top of a clear hierarchy, and his or her strength and authority remained largely unchallenged.

CEOs' pay mirrored that power. Fiorina brought home an annual paycheck that was 20 times that of President George Bush. In her leisure time, she cruised on her large, private yacht.

Particularly in the United States, CEOs like Fiorina were used to getting their way. Technically, they were appointed by, and reported to, their boards of directors. But many, like Fiorina, held the title of Chairman of the Board as well as Chief Executive. They set the board's agenda and controlled much of the board's access to information. They benefited from a business culture, developed during the 20th century, that held that strong, even autocratic, CEOs offered the best route to business success. The successful CEO wasn't first among equals; the CEO was boss.

In Fiorina's case, this position of power was particularly sweet because she was a woman. The ranks of corporate power, far more than the ranks of political power, had remained the province of men throughout the 20th century. When the elite members of the Business Council held their regular meetings, there were seldom more than one or two women in the crowded room—or for that matter, more than one or two African Americans. In recent years, a few prominent women, like Meg Whitman of eBay Inc. or Anne Mulcahy of Xerox Corporation or Andrea Jung of Avon Products, had broken through the glass ceiling and made it to the top. But at the beginning of 2005, those women were still scarce enough to be counted on the fingers of two hands. Among Fortune 500 companies, no more than 10 had female CEOs.

Testosterone ran particularly strong in the telecommunications world, where Fiorina made her career. In spite of its nickname, "Ma Bell" and her progeny were overwhelmingly male enterprises. As a young executive at Lucent, an offshoot of AT&T, she suffered the indignity of a boss who once introduced her as "our token bimbo." ("You will never do that to me again," she told him afterward.) She had once attended an all-male sales lunch at a club where scantily dressed women danced on the tops of tables. Her male colleagues had suggested she skip the lunch, which they had arranged, but she refused, arriving in her most serious-looking business attire. The dancers said they wouldn't dance at the table "until the lady leaves." Later, when Lucent bought Ascend Communications—a company with a legendary cowboy culture—some at Ascend were critical of their new acquirers, saying the Lucent sales force "didn't have any balls." Fiorina appeared onstage at the first joint sales meeting in cowboy boots and with a pair of her husband's socks stuffed in the crotch of her pants, declaring to the stunned Ascend team, "Our balls are as big as anyone's in this room."

But for Carly, that was all in the past. Now she sat where the men had sat before her. She enjoyed the pay and the perks and, most important, the power that came with the job of chairman of the board and chief executive officer of one of the world's great corporations. She had triumphed in a man's world.

Or so she thought.

But on January 10, 2005, that world was changing.

Without Fiorina's knowledge, members of her board of directors had held a series of highly unusual telephone conversations in December and early January to discuss their dissatisfaction with her leadership.

The company certainly had its problems. Its stock was flagging—

55 percent below where it had been when Carly took over in 1999. And it had failed to meet its financial projections for the third quarter of 2004, which ended July 31—prompting complaints from Wall Street analysts. Neither problem suggested crisis. All technology stocks were trading well below their breathless levels of 1999, and many companies occasionally missed their financial targets. Indeed, Fiorina liked to point out that before she took over, HP had missed Wall Street's earnings expectations for nine quarters straight. Moreover, she had acted quickly to address the third quarter situation—firing three top sales executives whom she blamed for the miss, and coming up with a plan for moving forward.

Still, some of the directors were increasingly uneasy. They had problems with Fiorina's management style. The firing of the sales executives, they thought, had been clumsily executed, and seemed designed to absolve her of any responsibility for the third quarter miss. Moreover, Carly had become imperious, they thought—disdainful of the analysts on Wall Street who criticized her, disdainful of her employees and fellow executives. She had centralized power in her office, then gone off making speeches and traveling so often that some of her own team complained she wasn't available when decisions had to be made. Members of the board wanted her to delegate more power to some of her top executives, or bring in new ones. Whenever they suggested that, however, she responded with icy silence.

Most important, the directors felt Fiorina was disdainful of them. In the wake of the corporate scandals, all boards were under pressure to take their jobs seriously. But Fiorina, they felt, wasn't willing to take their concerns seriously. She didn't want to be influenced by them.

So finally, the board decided to send a delegation of three directors to have a serious talk with Carly, and detail their concerns. A meeting was set for the afternoon of January 10.

Imperiousness, arrogance, reluctance to share power—these sins of Carly Fiorina's were hardly unknown among the CEOs of corporate America. At times, they even seemed to be requisites of the job. In the past, they hardly would have been sufficient crimes to spur a board to fire the CEO. Boards of big companies had tended to be close, clubby affairs—filled with the friends and associates of the CEO, and prone to act only when absolutely necessary.

But the seismic plates under the corporate landscape were shifting. And Carly Fiorina was about to become a victim.

2 ||||||||||||||||||||||||||||||||||

If any CEO ever deserved the adjective "imperial," it was Hank Greenberg. As 2005 began, he had been CEO of American International Group for three remarkable decades, building his company from an obscure, second-tier insurer to the largest insurance company in the world, with revenues of $100 billion.

The 79-year-old Greenberg ruled AIG like his personal fiefdom, with absolute authority. He was a hands-on manager, likely to get involved in any part of his sprawling business at any time. And when he did, there was no questioning his judgment.

His power extended beyond the confines of his company. He consorted with leaders of government around the world, advising them on how to do their jobs even as he was seeking their help in doing his. His company's extraordinary generosity to think tanks as well as political campaigns gave him instant entrée to all the most powerful players in Washington, and he used that entrée liberally. Through most of his career, his reputation was not that of someone who *broke* the rules; rather, of someone who *made* the rules. He had played a major role in writing the tax laws governing investments in Bermuda, where some of his company's most important operations were based. According to Chinese officials, he personally negotiated the final details of the historic 2001 agreement that allowed China into the World Trade Organization (and allowed AIG to continue running wholly owned subsidiaries in China). As for the government regulators watching over his enterprise—well, as one former Securities and Exchange Commission official put it—Hank Greenberg never hesitated to call.

Hank Greenberg was a fighter. He had fought his way to the top. His father had owned a candy store on New York's Lower East Side, and died when Hank was just five. His mother remarried a dairy farmer, who lived in upstate New York, and Hank grew up milking cows before dawn each day.

He enlisted in the U.S. Army in 1942, at age 17—using a fake birth certificate to circumvent the requirement that enlistees be at least 18. He was part of the invasion force that landed at Omaha Beach in Normandy, and part of the force that later liberated the Dachau concentration camp.

After the army, he joined an obscure insurance company, American International Group, that had its roots in Shanghai, China, where it had been started by Cornelius Vander Starr. Impressed by Greenberg, Starr put him in charge of U.S. operations in 1962, and Greenberg began to expand rapidly the company's business through the use of insurance brokers, rather than costly agents. In 1968, at a dramatic meeting in Bermuda, Starr named the ambitious Greenberg as his successor, to the surprise and dismay of many longtime AIG executives. In 1969, Greenberg took the company public.

Greenberg fashioned himself as the ultimate risk taker, going where other insurance companies dared not go—selling kidnapping and ransom coverage, for instance, or insuring against earthquakes and floods or writing policies for oil rigs and satellites. He traveled the globe, building up such a deep network of contacts that Ronald Reagan's administration once offered him a top spot at the CIA. He was a fierce competitor, not only in business, but also in winning the allegiance and cooperation of governments. He behaved and was treated like a head of state. Indeed, AIG was very much like a sovereign nation, with its own diplomatic arrangements, its own economic rules, and with one man very clearly in charge.

For the shareholders of his company, the results could not have been better. Under his guidance, AIG's market value rose from $300 million to $170 billion. Its share price had tripled in the previous decade alone.

Even at 79 years old, Greenberg was a model of mental and physical fitness. He lunched daily on seafood and vegetables, worked out regularly on his StairMaster, and was an avid tennis player and skier. His employees knew he was loyal, but also ruthless. Mistakes weren't tolerated. He had his own elevator, guarded by his own security detail. At some meetings, Greenberg's butler would serve him hot tea in a china cup, and serve the others nothing. Executives traveling with him had to use the small pilot bathroom in the front of the corporate jet; the large fancy one in the back was reserved for Greenberg, his wife and their Maltese dog, Snowball.

For a while, Greenberg attempted to make his empire a dynasty. He had two sons in the business—Jeffrey and Evan. Jeffrey was the older, and had responded to his father's relentless expectations by becoming a perfectionist. A track star at Choate, and a graduate of Brown University and Georgetown Law, he set out to work outside his father's empire. Evan responded by dropping out. He ran away from a series of boarding schools, ending up at Stockbridge, an alternative school for troubled children of wealthy families. After that, he became a drifter, working as a cook and bartender in Colorado.

Both sons were eventually lured back to AIG, where they found that their father held them to an even higher standard than he set for their peers. He wouldn't hestitate to berate Jeffrey and Evan in front of others. They rankled under the pressure, and eventually both left, after it became clear to them that their father had no intention of retiring. Jeffrey left in 1995, after his onetime drifter brother Evan was given equal status in the company. Evan left in 2000. Both went on to run other companies in the insurance business.

Greenberg paid himself lavishly for his efforts—$7.5 million cash in 2003, plus options valued at $26.2 million. There was no accounting for the many perks that went with the office. He vacationed at an AIG-owned resort in Vermont, or on a yacht owned by an AIG-related company and kept in Florida. In his mind, there was no clear division between what belonged to the company and what belonged to him. And he was accountable to no one. Or so he thought.

He had a board of directors, of course, but it was a board whose members he had handpicked. He liked bringing on once-powerful people from Washington, as a way of cementing his influence there. President Ronald Reagan's top economic adviser, Martin Feldstein, was a member, as was President George H. W. Bush's top trade negotiator, Carla Hills, and President Bill Clinton's defense secretary, Bill Cohen. Also on the board was former UN ambassador Richard Holbrooke, who was widely thought to be in line for the secretary of state job in the next Democratic presidential administration.

Board members were treated lavishly. A seat on the AIG board was considered a plum assignment, in part because it was easy—under Greenberg, the company was a perennial success—and in part because the pay and perquisites were so generous. In 2005, a director received a $40,000 annual retainer, plus an additional $5,000 per committee he or she served on. On top of that, directors were given

500 shares of AIG stock, worth another $30,000 or so, and an option to buy another 2,500 shares at a fixed price, earning them another $25,000 if the stock increased by $10.

One of the biggest benefits of being on the AIG board came from the generous charitable contributions made by the Starr Foundation, named after AIG's founder, C. V. Starr. In theory, the foundation was independent from the company. But in fact, Greenberg was its chairman, and used the contributions to extend his power and reach.

Ellen Futter, for instance, had been a director of AIG since 1999, and sat on the committee that determined Greenberg's compensation. She was also president of the American Museum of Natural History. The year she joined the board, the Starr Foundation committed $10 million over two years to build the museum's C. V. Starr Natural Science Building. Greenberg's personal foundation gave $50,000 to the museum in 2002 and 2003.

Richard Holbrooke, former U.S. ambassador to the United Nations, became an AIG director in 2001. He also served as chairman of the Asia Society, which was heavily supported by AIG. In 2005, the company paid a total of $539,743 to the Society.

After the scandals at Enron and WorldCom, when public companies came under pressure to name "lead" or "presiding" directors to help guide the board's deliberations, Greenberg turned to the person on the board he trusted most: Frank Zarb, the former head of the National Association of Securities Dealers. Greenberg didn't like the idea that someone other than he would have a leadership seat at the board table. He particularly didn't like the idea that the board would meet in "executive" session, without him present. In fact, Greenberg thought the whole idea of independent directors was a bit silly. With Zarb in the lead role, though, Greenberg could at least take comfort that he had a longtime friend and business partner leading the boardroom discussions.

In the wake of the problems at Enron and WorldCom and Tyco, AIG also came under the scrutiny of regulators. The scandals had embarrassed the Securities and Exchange Commission, and left them with more resources and more determination than ever to crack down on corporate accounting shenanigans. In 2002, they began looking into PNC Financial Services Group, which had entered into transactions with AIG designed to get $762 million in underperforming loans and volatile venture capital investments off PNC's books. The transactions looked suspiciously like those that had been used by Enron to clean up its books. They were accounting shams.

Then in 2003, the SEC accused a small Indiana cell phone distributor, Brightpoint, of goosing its profits with a sham insurance policy, also supplied by AIG. In this case, the insurance company was found to have backdated the policy, and to have given a misleading explanation of its purpose. Moreover, the SEC publicly chastised AIG for dragging its feet in response to the agency's requests for documents. AIG neither admitted nor denied wrongdoing, but agreed to pay a $10 million fine.

The regulators continued to look into AIG's affairs, as the investigations into PNC and Brightpoint expanded. In August of 2004, the company's lawyers, led by Ernest Patrikis, thought they had finally reached a settlement that would get the SEC off their backs. A key aspect of the deal was that AIG would allow an independent monitor into the company, with broad leeway to monitor transactions. On a Friday in August, the deal was all ready to be signed, and a press release had been prepared.

On Saturday morning, however, Greenberg called Patrikis and said the deal was off. He had had second thoughts. He wasn't going to allow a monitor into his company. What would AIG's customers think, if their information was subject to that kind of scrutiny? Tell the SEC to forget it, he said.

Always the fighter, Greenberg wasn't ready to give up.

Greenberg's action put the regulators on the warpath. On September 22, the SEC put out a statement warning AIG that it could face civil action over its transactions with PNC. A week later, the company said it had been warned by the Department of Justice it was also the target of a criminal investigation into the same matter. And a few days later, the company revealed it was being investigated by government officials for issuing news releases suggesting, incorrectly, that the government's concerns were limited to PNC transactions—when in fact the company knew the SEC was investigating a series of other transactions.

Greenberg was unrepentant. He had dealt with plenty of regulators in the past. And he had found that his money and his connections were enough to keep them in check. If they started down a path he didn't approve of, a phone call from him was usually enough to turn them around.

So he continued to drag his feet in the investigations. He even went so far as to hire a public relations firm that offered to pay financial industry experts if they would criticize New York attorney general Eliot Spitzer—although the company said it never actually authorized that effort. In his public comments, Greenberg was unrestrained, attacking the regulatory excesses occurring in the wake of the corporate scandals. "The cumulative effect of these measures has had a chilling effect on the economy," he said at one dinner. "Regulatory overexuberance has the potential to do real harm to the economy."

Harm to the economy, yes. But harm to Hank Greenberg? At 79 years old, in spite of his problems, he acted as invincible as ever. The world may have changed. But Hank Greenberg hadn't yet.

3 ▍▍▍▍▍▍▍▍▍▍▍▍▍▍▍▍▍▍▍▍▍▍▍▍▍▍

On Sunday, February 27, 2005, the board of directors of the Boeing Company gathered for a meeting at the Ritz-Carlton in Huntington, California.

Spirits were high. The scandal-rocked airline company, which dominates the market for large aircraft, finally seemed to be getting its act together. Two days earlier, the U.S. government had lifted its restriction on doing new business with Boeing, praising the efforts of current management to clean up the place. And the stock price was up, showing that investors had confidence in management as well.

The board had been through some tough times together. Boeing, which got more than half its $52 billion in annual revenues by selling to the Pentagon, had suffered a string of serious scandals in Washington. First, the U.S. Air Force had stripped Boeing of $1 billion in rocket-launch work after investigators found the company used inside information on rivals to win contracts. That was the case that led the government to suspend Boeing from bidding on new business.

Then, the company's former chief financial officer, Michael Sears, was found to have dangled a job offer before an Air Force acquisitions official, Darleen Druyun, who had influenced government contracts for Boeing worth more than $6 billion. In the wake of the scandal, Sears and Druyun were fired. And faced with the threat of losing critical government business, the Boeing board dismissed the company's chief executive officer, Phil Condit, as well.

That was just 15 months earlier. To replace Condit, the board had called a former Boeing executive, Harry Stonecipher, age 67, out of retirement.

Stonecipher was a central casting, Horatio Alger sort of CEO—gruff, earthy, direct, all business, no nonsense. And the board loved him. The son of a Tennessee coal miner, he started working at a 24-hour truck stop when he was just 11 years old. He dropped out of college in 1955 to work in the General Motors Corporation's aircraft-engine division. Then after earning a degree at Tennessee Technological University, he worked his way up through the General Electric Company's aircraft-engine unit. Widely admired, he became chief executive of aircraft component maker Sundstrand, then chief executive of the McDonnell Douglas Corporation. After McDonnell Douglas merged with Boeing in 1997, he served as vice chairman and president of Boeing until his retirement in 2002. From modest beginnings, he had become Boeing's second-largest individual shareholder, with a stake worth $72 million.

Eager to get Boeing out from under the cloud of scandal, he made ethics a priority. He hired a former colleague from McDonnell Douglas, Bonnie Soodik, to head up a new ethics office that would set policies, conduct training and monitor compliance. When Soodik told Stonecipher she'd have the ethics policy ready for him in four months, Stonecipher interrupted: "Maybe you didn't understand me. You're looking at your calendar. I'm looking at my watch." The materials went out within a month.

Stonecipher made it clear to everyone at Boeing that ethics were his top priority. Shortly after taking office, an interviewer for *USA Today* asked him: "What's your first order of business?" Stonecipher responded: "Restore the great reputation that Boeing has enjoyed in the past. It's been a little tarnished recently, so I've been spending an awful lot of my time working on that."

Stonecipher also emphasized that ethics had to start at the top. When one employee challenged him by saying, "It really aggravates the hell out of me that we're all signing this code of conduct all around here when all the trouble is at the top of the company," Stonecipher responded that he would deal with the problem at the top. In an interview with the *Wall Street Journal,* Stonecipher said: "You can rest assured that we will investigate every tip, and if we find out that somebody did something they shouldn't have, we will deal with it swiftly and summarily."

Stonecipher's approach seemed to be working. On the Friday before the board meeting, when the government lifted its 20-month-long suspension on doing new business with the company, Acting Air Force Secretary Peter Teets cited Stonecipher's work to rebuild the company's reputation as one reason for the action. Meanwhile, the company's stock price had climbed more than 30 percent since Stonecipher had taken over.

So the board had reason to feel satisfied when they gathered in February. Kenneth Duberstein, former White House chief of staff under President Ronald Reagan, chaired the board's compensation committee meeting that Sunday afternoon. All felt Stonecipher and his team were doing an excellent job, and voted to give them hefty bonuses.

Leaving the committee meeting, Duberstein got on a hotel elevator with Lewis Platt, who had preceded Carly Fiorina as chief executive of Hewlett-Packard and was now the nonexecutive chairman of the board at Boeing. While Duberstein seemed cheery, Platt looked deeply disturbed.

"What's the matter?" Duberstein asked. "I thought that went well."

"You just wait," Platt replied.

He then told Duberstein that he had been given an anonymous letter—sent to him, Boeing's general counsel, and to Soodik—alleging that Stonecipher was having an affair with one of the company's executives, Debra Peabody, a 48-year-old executive in Boeing's Washington office. The letter also implied that Peabody's career had been helped as a result.

Included in the letter were five days' worth of e-mails between Stonecipher and Peabody. Some of them appeared to have been sent by BlackBerry, during the workday. They were stunningly graphic—using raw language to talk about his desire for her.

"We are going to have a very interesting dinner tonight," Platt said.

The board reassembled for cocktails with Boeing's senior managers, then went off to a working dinner that was to include board members only. At the dinner, Platt asked Stonecipher to leave. Then he read the letter to the board, and portions of the e-mails. He left out some of the most graphic passages, embarrassed to read them with female board members—like former assistant secretary of state Rozanne Ridgeway—in the room. But everyone got the idea—and all were shocked.

There are no books, no studies, no records, telling how often CEOs have engaged in extramarital relations with employees. But you don't have to pursue this issue very far to conclude the answer is: A lot. Power is an aphrodisiac, for both sides of a relationship. For the powerful, it creates a sense of possibility and entitlement. For the less powerful, well, the magnetic attraction is obvious.

Occasionally, these relationships had broken into public view. In June of 1991, for instance, a gossip columnist for the *New York Daily News* reported that Citicorp chief executive John Reed was having an affair with one of the stewardesses on his corporate jet—a woman he later married. In 1999, the *Harvard Business Review* published a case study of a fictitious company whose chief executive was cheating on his wife with a younger employee. That case study was written by Suzy Wetlaufer, who later had a notorious extramarital affair with Stonecipher's former boss, General Electric chairman Jack Welch. The two are now married.

But while such affairs could cause great embarrassment, they seldom cost a CEO his job. More often, when such a case came to light, it was swept under the rug—even if the sweeping required a payoff to an injured lover. Indeed, Stonecipher's predecessor, Phil Condit—whose fourth marriage was to a former colleague—was rumored to have gotten into similar trouble, with the board's knowledge. In an interview shortly before he died, Lewis Platt refused to provide details. But he said that with Condit, "we passed on some things we wouldn't have today."

Now, however, things were different. Boeing was in the midst of a massive struggle to restore its reputation, and had made ethics a priority. Stonecipher, meanwhile, had been astonishingly careless, detailing the affair in e-mail messages that the board feared, could soon become public. Platt didn't know who had sent those messages. But if the board failed to act, what would stop that person from sending the same messages to the press?

When dinner ended, board members returned to their rooms, each left alone to contemplate the problem that they would have to address as a group the next day. None of them knew yet how this would turn out. But for another powerful CEO, the writing was on the wall.

From their very beginnings, corporations were political institutions.

The people who run today's large companies don't like to think of themselves that way. They are quick to claim they are above politics. They are part of the "free market"—actors in Adam Smith's great commercial drama, pursuing their enlightened self-interest while the "invisible hand" guides them toward the betterment of society.

But that ignores both fact and history. The truth is, Adam Smith, author of *The Wealth of Nations,* disapproved of corporations. His free-market economy was atomistic—individuals or small businesses contracting with each other in countless transactions that, together, made up the marketplace.

Corporations were something else entirely. They were usually chartered by the government, granted special legal protections, and often given monopoly rights. They were not just players in the marketplace; their purpose was to *subsume* large portions of the marketplace, replacing the decisions made by freely contracting individuals and small businesses with decisions made by corporate leaders, whose power was delegated from the top. Among other things, Smith worried about what later came to be known as the "agency" problem—hired managers whose motives and vigilance would be different from those of people who actually owned and supplied capital to the business.

In their early days, companies were direct extensions of government. The Dutch East India Company, for instance, was established in 1602 with a state-sanctioned monopoly over Dutch trade with the countries of the east. The English East India Company had a similar monopoly, and eventually grew into a private empire, ruling India with its own army of 260,000 native troops—twice the size of the British army. Hudson's Bay Company, founded in 1670, oversaw British trade with the New World. John Law's Mississippi Company was chartered by France in 1716 and given power to issue banknotes, in a desperate but misguided effort to cure that country's inflation problem. Over time, Law also won the charter to oversee French trade with the New World, and attempted in 1719 to convert the entire national debt into Mississippi Company shares.

These kinds of companies were seen as necessary by the state because of the vast scope of their undertakings. Equipping a fleet of ships for a journey of months, if not years, required more capital than any private citizen, or partnership of citizens, or even a monarch, could muster. "Joint-stock" companies were created to pool the capital necessary to finance these bold ventures, usually overseas. Over time, the joint-stock companies were also given special legal protections, so that no individual investor could be held liable for the acts of the corporations, which were engaged in highly risky enterprises.

Since investors could not be held liable, the companies themselves were gradually given the rights and responsibilities of "persons" under the law. The limited-liability, joint-stock company took on a life of its own, enabling it to last long beyond the life span of any of its founders or investors. The English East India Company, for instance, survived for 274 years. Hudson's Bay Company still exists today.

Periodic and spectacular scandals caused support for these new creations to ebb and flow over much of the 17th and 18th centuries. After gaining control of France's trade flows and money supply, John Law's Mississippi Company sparked a speculative boom followed by a frenetic bust, forcing Law to flee the country in December 1720 as it sank into economic chaos. The same year, the South Sea Company took over Britain's national debt, sold shares, and watched its share price skyrocket. To prevent competition, the company succeeded in convincing Parliament to pass the "Bubble Act," which made it extremely difficult to set up new joint-stock companies, only to then watch the South Sea Company collapse and eventually be nationalized. The Bubble Act wasn't repealed for a century.

The next great impetus to joint-stock companies came from the construction of canals and railroads—vast efforts that required huge investments of capital not easily raised from a single source. And as the corporate form became more common, the legal system evolved to accommodate it. In Britain, the Joint Stock Companies Act of 1856, later revised and expanded in the Companies Act of 1862, set the stage for the explosion. While companies still needed a government charter, the issuance of charters became routine, and thousands of new companies sprang into existence.

In the United States, where vast distances separated major cities, the railroads became the driving force behind corporate expansion—and also led to one of the first great corporate scandals of the New World, the Crédit Mobilier scandal. Not surprisingly, at the heart of that scandal was collusion between business and government. Nevertheless, railroads continued to expand and consolidate under the protection of the corporate form.

Similar consolidation happened in the retail business, thanks to Sears and Roebuck, as well as steel, tobacco, and most famously, oil, so that by the beginning of the 20th century, the U.S. economy was largely in the hands of great captains of industry, who came to be known as "robber barons." They benefited from a legal tradition in the United States that gave the power over corporate charters to states. Eager to have great companies "reside" within their borders, the states competed to provide lenient corporate laws. In 1901, it was New Jersey that was winning this legal "race to the bottom" to provide lenient laws, with two-thirds of all American firms with capital of $10 million or more incorporated in that state. A generation later, tiny Delaware had gone even further in catering to corporate interests, and became the charter home for thousands of large American companies—a distinction it retains today. Most of the largest companies in the country are chartered in the state.

At the turn of the century, many large companies were run by founders and owners—like John D. Rockefeller at Standard Oil, or Henry Ford of Ford Motors. But by the 1920s, a different sort of leader was on the rise, typified by Alfred Sloan, who became the president of General Motors in 1923. Sloan was not an entrepreneur, like Henry Ford; he was a manager. He came to symbolize the new science of management. By 1929, his company had surpassed Ford's in sales, ushering in the era of the manager. Business schools and management consultants began to sprout and grow, offering their ideas about how to organize human beings in the most productive fashion.

What emerged was an economy very different from the market-driven one imagined by Adam Smith. This economy wasn't composed of thousands of small businesses acting in their own self-interest. It was made up of a relatively small number of large corporations run by managers financed by other people's money. In Adam Smith's world, self-interest provided the motivation to make the system work, and the market allocated resources. In Alfred Sloan's world, management filled that role, providing overall direction to large swaths of the economy.

■

The extraordinary strength of the corporate system was evident in the burgeoning U.S. economy of the early 20th century. The rise of the corporation in many ways mirrored the rise of U.S. economic dominance in the world.

But there was an inherent weakness, as well, first diagnosed by Adolf Berle and Gardiner Means in their landmark 1932 study *The Modern Corporation and Private Property*. The book documented the fact that, since the Civil War, corporations had come to dominate economic life in the United States, and that their power was increasingly concentrated. The 200 largest companies controlled half the nation's corporate wealth. It went on to point out that increasingly, these giant companies were run by "persons other than those who have ventured their own wealth" for the enterprise.

It was this last point that turned out to be the most important.

Concentrations of wealth were nothing new in society. But the modern corporation had turned control of vast pools of wealth over to corporate managers, who in turn exercised immense power. Because these companies operated, more often than not, under rules established by the lax courts of Delaware, their power was largely unchecked. The only real recourse an investor had, in most cases, was to withdraw his money.

"The separation of ownership from control," wrote Berle and Means,

> produces a condition where the interests of owner and of ultimate manager may, and often do, diverge, and where many of the checks which formerly operated to limit the use of power disappeared. Size alone tends to give these giant corporations a social significance not attached to the smaller units of private enterprise. . . . In creating these new relationships, quasi-public corporation may fairly be said to work a revolution.

The essence of that revolution was separating wealth from the power that would normally go along with it.

> The economic power in the hands of the few persons who control a giant corporation is a tremendous force which can harm or benefit a multitude of individuals, affect whole districts, shift the currents of trade, bring ruin to one community and prosperity to another. The organizations which they control have passed far beyond the realm of private enterprise—they have become more nearly social institutions.

Berle and Means had found the central paradox of the modern corporation. They were established primarily to make money. Yet they had become large social and political institutions. As such, they depended on the goodwill of the public to survive.

If anyone doubted that fact, the years following the publication of Berle and Means's book demonstrated its truth. The excesses of the 1920s, followed by the bust of the 1930s, caused corporations to lose their public support. They became targets of public anger. Democratic president Franklin Roosevelt responded with a series of laws greatly increasing the government's regulation of business. The most important of those laws were the 1933 Securities Act and the 1934 Securities Exchange Act, which established the Securities and Exchange Commission and codified the public's interest in keeping an eye on corporate activities.

While the 1930s was a period of great cynicism about business, the law itself was relatively modest. Its principal goal was not to limit the activities of corporations, but to increase transparency, so investors could get a clearer idea of what was happening with their money. The essential conservatism of that approach was reinforced by the man whom Roosevelt chose to become the first chairman of the Securities and Exchange Commission—Joseph P. Kennedy.

Kennedy was a financier who had been involved in his share of financial scandals in the 1920s. New Deal liberal Jerome Frank compared the appointment to "setting a wolf to guard a flock of sheep." But Kennedy's conservatism underscored Roosevelt's pragmatism. The agency he headed, instead of attacking corporations, served to protect corporations from the public anger, and helped reassure both businesses and investors, clearing the way for the next great expansion of corporate power.

In the end, however, it was not Joe Kennedy who restored public support for large corporations: it was World War II. The quarter century that followed the end of that war marked the heyday of corporate power.

No one symbolized the new age of corporate power more than Harold Geneen, the chief executive of the International Telephone and Telegraph Corporation—known to most as simply ITT. An accountant by training, Geneen traded on his expertise at management controls to climb his way up the corporate ladder, and in 1959, win the top job at the global telephone manufacturing and operating company. He took control with an iron fist and turned ITT into an acquisition machine, building a sprawling, multi-industry, global conglomerate. His power was felt not just in business, but in government, both at home and in Europe and Latin America. Indeed, he ultimately achieved infamy for his involvement in two prominent scandals—one involving ITT's role in financing Richard Nixon's 1972 GOP convention, the other involving a joint effort with the Central Intelligence Agency to keep socialist Salvador Allende Gossens out of power in Chile.

His power over the company and its wide-ranging affairs seemed close to absolute. A common joke at ITT was about the pronunciation of his last name—was it a hard g as in "God," or a soft g as in "Jesus"? Because his empire had so many far-flung businesses—it started with telecommunications, but spread to Avis Rent-a-Car, Sheraton hotels, and a host of other unrelated businesses—he delegated authority broadly. But he was famed for drilling his executives on the details of their businesses. His frequent meetings in Brussels were held on New York time, to suit his biological clock. He worked countless hours, and expected others to do the same. He once called a review session for the day before Thanksgiving, and blithely ignored polite suggestions late in the day that executives had planes to catch. At 8 p.m., he was reminded again, and kept going. The meeting lasted until 1 a.m. Executives who dared to challenge his authority frequently found themselves without a job.

He did, of course, have a board of directors, which had hired him and to which he was, in theory, accountable. He worried a great

deal about the board and what members were thinking, and he prohibited other ITT executives from speaking to directors without his
knowledge. He wanted to control all communications with his
board.

In 1963, Robert McKinney, John F. Kennedy's ambassador to
Switzerland, joined the ITT board, and began to question Geneen's
strategy of acquiring unrelated, and often not terribly successful,
businesses. The following year, he began to talk to other directors
about the board's need for a strong chairman, who could keep the
chief executive in check. Geneen fought back, confronting McKinney, showing him that he had a majority of directors on his side.
McKinney ultimately resigned, and Geneen moved that he be made
chairman, as well as chief executive. The board went along.

Even after the scandals captured public attention and weakened
Geneen, his rule continued unchecked. But in 1977, the board finally insisted the 67-year-old executive step aside for a new chief
executive, allowing Geneen to stay on as chairman. When the board
refused to take his advice on a successor, Geneen maneuvered to
make sure their pick, Lyman Hamilton, was fired just a year and a
half after assuming control.

The great power of corporations in this third quarter of the
20th century was captured in an important book by Harvard academic John Kenneth Galbraith called *The New Industrial State*.
In Galbraith's view, large corporations controlled much of what
happened in the economies of the Western world. He argued
that these companies were the equivalent of the Soviet planning
agency: they would decide what products to make, then use their
advertising and marketing clout to create the demand for those
products.

"We have an economic system which, whatever its formal ideological billing, is in substantial part a planned economy," Galbraith
wrote.

The initiative in deciding what is to be produced comes not from the sovereign consumer who, through the market, issues the instructions that bend the productive mechanism to his ultimate will. Rather it comes from the great producing organization which reaches forward to control the customer to its needs.

As a portrait of economic life at the time it was written, Galbraith's book was a classic. But as a prediction of the future, it failed miserably. Because even as Galbraith was writing, the economy was beginning to undergo a profound transition—the result of changes in technology, changes in capital markets and changes in government policy.

In Galbraith's view, technology was increasing the power of corporations. As he saw it, the increasing complexity of goods and the long lead times necessary to produce them required large companies to become ever more skilled in planning, and to make planning decisions long before testing their goods in the market.

But in fact, a revolution in information technology helped to bring companies much closer to the marketplace, providing them faster access to information on what consumers were demanding, and giving them greater ability to adjust to those demands. Improvements in transportation and the downsizing of products were making markets increasingly global and thus more competitive. If companies acted the way Galbraith imagined—planning their output without regard for the consumer, assuming they had the marketing skill to sell whatever they made—they ran the risk of being clobbered by more nimble competition from overseas.

Moreover, the late 1970s and early 1980s saw the rise of government policies that served to strengthen these trends. In the last 25 years of the 20th century, there was a remarkable burst of deregulation and privatization, and a freeing of market forces that served to undercut whatever power corporations had to "plan" the economy. It was a period of what the economist Joseph Schumpeter called "creative destruction." Powerful new corporations—like Microsoft— sprang up from nowhere, while older companies that failed to keep up with the times—Westinghouse Electric, for instance—disappeared from the scene. The people who ran large companies might still have had immense power, but if they didn't pay attention to the signals from the market, they could find that power rapidly eroding beneath them.

Capital markets changed, too. The ownership of corporations became increasingly democratic, with more and more Americans owning stock, either directly or through their pension funds. Large pension funds became major owners of companies, creating what Peter Drucker called in his 1976 book *The Unseen Revolution* a sort of pension fund socialism. Meanwhile, those pension funds, as well as other shareholders, began to ask for a greater say in the company's actions.

By the 1980s and 1990s, the CEOs of big companies were living in a very different world than the one inhabited by Harold Geneen. They faced challenges from corporate raiders, like Carl Icahn, and from buyout firms that sought to undermine the management of companies that weren't serving shareholder interests. They also faced increasing demands from shareholders, on issues ranging from investments in Africa to their policies on the environment.

But through the end of the century, corporations and their leaders still enjoyed widespread support and praise from the public. While democracy was rapidly spreading to governments around the world, corporate democracy remained largely a myth. The autocratic CEO was still a staple in American business, and leaders like General Electric's Jack Welch enjoyed superstar status. Moreover, the surging bull market of the 1980s and 1990s reinforced their status, as more and more Americans were able to enjoy the fruits of their success, through 401(k)s and other investment vehicles.

At the turn of the millennium, it was these business leaders who were the world's most powerful leaders. The chief executive officer—a title barely known 100 years earlier—had ascended to the top of the social pyramid, and viewed the world from Olympian heights.

Time magazine's celebrated annual Person of the Year demonstrated the trend. The award was created to honor the most influential figure each year. Businessmen won the honor in 1928 and 1929—when the award went to automaker Walter Chrysler and Owen Young of General Electric. But not a single business leader won the honor from 1930 to 1990—instead, it went to political leaders like Gandhi, Franklin Roosevelt, Adolf Hitler, Joseph Stalin, Harry Truman and John F. Kennedy; or to social leaders like Dr. Martin Luther King Jr., Pope John XXII and the astronauts.

But in the 1990s, the CEOs had taken over. Three of them graced *Time*'s honored list that decade—Ted Turner of CNN in 1991, Andy Grove of Intel in 1997 and Jeff Bezos of Amazon in 1999. In between, countless others—Michael Eisner of Disney, Steve Jobs of Apple, Steve Case of AOL, Bill Gates of Microsoft, Sam Walton of Wal-Mart, and the heads of all three U.S. auto companies—made the magazine's cover. With the markets soaring, CEOs were heroes.

I spent the final hours of 1999 with my family at the home of Lawrence Summers, who stood as a testament to the extraordinary nature of that millennial moment. As President Bill Clinton's treasury secretary, Summers represented the new consensus that had emerged with regard to government economic policy.

Summers was a Democrat by temperament, with a strong preference for policies that promoted social justice. But he was an econ-omist by training, with a deep respect for the power of markets, and a deep understanding of how and why government efforts to over-ride those markets so often failed. Like his predecessor in the job, Robert Rubin, he had helped lead the Clinton administration to adopt policies that embraced the free market, celebrated business, and recognized that government's role in the economy was impor-tant, but limited.

Rubin and Summers had made common cause with a long-time conservative Republican, Federal Reserve chairman Alan Greenspan, to help spread the principles of capitalism around the globe. They had used international institutions like the International Monetary Fund and the World Trade Organization to prod other countries to open their markets, roll back regulation, privatize gov-ernment-owned enterprises, and embrace market ideology. *Time* magazine had put the three of them on its cover, under a headline "The Committee to Save the World."

"The old debates were about what the role of the market was, what was the role of the state," Summers told author Dan Yergin in an interview for the PBS series *The Commanding Heights.* "I think it's now generally appreciated that it's the market that harnesses people's initiative best. And the real focus of progressive thinking is not how to oppose and suppress market forces but how to use mar-ket forces to achieve progressive objectives."

By the end of 1999, the great ideological debates of the cen-tury, between capitalism and communism throughout the world, or more narrowly, between Hooverite Republicans and Rooseveltian Democrats within this country, seemed to have been resolved. The gospel of free markets was accepted in most corners of the world. Deregulation and privatization and the minimization of gov-ernment influence in the economy had become widely accepted principles. The great global battle of ideas that had characterized the 20th century was over, and capitalism and democracy had won. It was, Francis Fukuyama argued, the "end of history." Or so it seemed.

The millennial moment, however, didn't last long. By the spring of 2000, the high-flying technology stocks began to stumble. The tech-heavy NASDAQ stock market climbed above 5,000 in the second week of March, then began a nosedive that caused it to lose more than half its value by year's end. Then came the terror attacks of September 11, 2001, with their four fateful airplanes, two crashing into the World Trade Center, one into the Pentagon and one into the farmland of central Pennsylvania. The attacks rattled the economy further, and quickly obliterated Fukuyama's naive notion that history had somehow ended.

On October 16, 2001, just one month after the terror attacks, the Enron Corporation, recently dubbed by *Fortune* magazine as the most innovative company in America, disclosed that it was taking a half-billion-dollar after-tax charge to its earnings because it was revising its accounting for some transactions it had made with one of its "special purpose entities." Those entities had been designed to remove some costs from the company's books, but on closer examination, it became clear they were shams. The announcement of the accounting revision hastened the company's downward spiral into litigation and bankruptcy. Enron employees, who had been encouraged by company management to keep all their savings in Enron stock, rather than in other assets, suddenly found that their retirement savings had disappeared. And Enron executives, who had liquidated their own generous options even as the company was going down, found themselves vilified.

It was clear that the world had suddenly changed. In short order, Congress created the first big new federal bureaucracy to come along in more than a quarter century—the Transportation Security Administration, whose job it was to assure safety at the nation's airports. It then proceeded to work on a sweeping rewrite of the securities laws that had been passed in the aftermath of the 1929 stock market crash.

That legislation, subsequently known as the Sarbanes-Oxley Act of 2002, began as a relatively mild effort to increase criminal penalties for executives who have misled the public and to create a new accounting industry watchdog. But as the bill was being negotiated in the spring and summer of 2002, a series of new corporate scandals exploded. Xerox had improperly accelerated revenues from long-term equipment leases; Qwest and Global Crossing had manipulated revenues and expenses on fiber-optic deals; cable firm Adelphia had apparently been looted by the family that controlled its shares; Tyco CEO Dennis Kozlowski had used shareholder money for a binge of excessive spending, including a lavish party in Sardinia and a $6,000 shower curtain. Finally, WorldCom, the telecommunications company, disclosed that it had falsely claimed billions of dollars' worth of ordinary expenses as assets, and collapsed into bankruptcy.

All of that prodded Congress to steadily ratchet up the proscriptions of Sarbanes-Oxley, which by the time it passed in late July was the biggest rewrite of laws affecting the securities industry since the 1930s.

The seismic changes in the economic landscape didn't end there. Regulators, flush with new resources, began an emboldened attack on corporate accounting schemes. And when the federal regulators let down their guard, New York's ambitious attorney general, Eliot Spitzer, was on hand to attack in their place. In the effort to restore confidence, industry groups like the New York Stock Exchange adopted new listing rules for companies, encouraging them to strengthen their boards with independent directors who met separately from management and oversaw the annual audit.

The change of mood in Washington, from the probusiness days of the late 1990s to the antibusiness fervor of 2002, was breathtaking to watch. Legislators who had been business's greatest friends in Washington—like Michael Oxley, who chaired the House Financial Services Committee—felt powerless to stand in the way of the strong, prevailing winds.

For those occupying the chief executive suite, it was a frightening time. The public had turned against them, and so had their close friends in Washington. During this period, I was hosting a nightly television show on CNBC called *Capital Report,* and the e-mail from viewers each night overflowed with contempt for their onetime business heroes. They felt betrayed, both by the disappearance of their own stock market wealth and the almost-daily reports of perfidy by executives.

We repeatedly invited CEOs to come on *Capital Report* and tell us why they felt the broad-brush backlash against them was unfair. Yet nearly all CEOs refused the invitation. They were facing a force they didn't comprehend, and their first instinct was to duck for cover. Their hope, no doubt, was that the storm would blow over.

But it didn't. It kept blowing harder. And by early 2005, it was ready to claim some victims. Carly Fiorina, Hank Greenberg and Harry Stonecipher were among the first on the list.

5 ||||||||||||||||||||||||||||||

The three people who called on Carly Fiorina on January 10, 2005—
Pattie Dunn, George Keyworth and Richard Hackborn—were all
members of her board of directors. In the world as taught in university classrooms, they were her bosses—the people to whom she reported and was accountable. In theory, they represented the
shareholders, who owned the company and employed her.

But that theory was very different from the reality that had grown
up around big corporations in the 20th century. Corporate boards,
in most cases, had a clubby feel. Their members were often handpicked by the CEO. Many were CEOs themselves. They provided
support, counsel and advice when asked. They were elected by the
shareholders, but the rules of shareholder elections were rigged in a
way that made it extremely difficult to elect anyone other than the
candidates proposed by management. While the CEO technically
reported to the board, the board, in the case of most American companies, was chaired by the chief executive—creating an odd, circu-
lar structure of accountability.

Fiorina met with the three in the Hewlett-Packard boardroom,
across the hall from her office on the first floor of the company's Palo
Alto, California, headquarters. They sat in a comfortable seating
area next to the table at which the board usually met, with windows
looking out onto a Japanese garden.

It was a tranquil setting. But it would not be a tranquil meeting.

Fiorina thought the meeting odd from the start. In two days,
the board would be having its annual strategy discussion at a

hotel in San Francisco. Why did these directors need to meet with her now?

Moreover, she was surprised by the directors who made up this small group. At the board's last meeting, she thought, they had agreed that another director, Robert Knowling, would handle communications with the CEO. Knowling was one of the few directors whom Fiorina had brought onto the board herself. He had explicitly said he was "signing on to Carly," not HP. He was clearly her closest ally on the board, yet he hadn't been included in this group.

Instead the group was led by Pattie Dunn, who had been a member of the board since 1998, when she was recruited by former CEO Lewis Platt. A former chief executive of Barclays Global Investors, the San Francisco–based money management firm, she had stepped down from that job a few years earlier to fight cancer. As she sat in the HP boardroom in January of 2005, she was in the midst of a brutal 20-month round of chemotherapy. She had never before played a leadership role on the board. Indeed, Fiorina later said Dunn's "opinions were frequently hard to discern."

■

Then there was George Keyworth, the former science adviser, who had been on the board since 1986, but had grown close to Fiorina during her years as chairman. She was one of the first people he'd called a year earlier when his wife died. She had given the eulogy at her funeral. And to help him battle the loneliness after his wife's death, Fiorina invited him to a series of meetings on the company's efforts to get into digital entertainment. During that time, Keyworth would pop into her office frequently to offer unsolicited advice. Maybe HP should buy Apple Computer, he'd suggest, or TiVo? She generally rejected that advice, and could see he was growing frustrated.

Fiorina was particularly surprised to see Keyworth and Dunn

acting in concert. In private, Keyworth, seldom short on opinions, had been brutally critical of Dunn. He complained that she didn't understand the company, and relied on process as a crutch. He frequently encouraged Fiorina to replace her.

Richard Hackborn's presence at the meeting was especially important. He had spent 33 years with HP, and held numerous top management jobs, including the position of chairman during the transition to Fiorina in 2000. He knew the organization well, and was highly respected by HP veterans. The company's founders had tried to get him to take the top job in the early 1990s, but he had turned them down. He played a critical role in agitating to get Lew Platt out of the top job, and in bringing Fiorina on board. He had briefly served as chairman, before the title was given to Fiorina. The fact that he was participating in this meeting showed it had to be taken seriously.

Pattie Dunn held a piece of paper, which had roughly 500 words typed out on it. What Fiorina didn't realize was that those words had been carefully negotiated during an extraordinary series of phone calls and e-mail exchanges over the preceding months. She had not been told of those meetings, or asked to participate in them.

Many analysts in the outside world thought Hewlett-Packard's problem was the merger with Compaq. The personal computer business was being commoditized by fierce competition and ruthless cost cutting, causing many to question why HP had ever wanted more of it. Scott McNealy of Sun Microsystem had called the merger "two garbage trucks colliding." Former HP CEO Lewis Platt compared it to a bad game of blackjack: "You never double down on 16."

But among board members, the merger was never questioned. Directors remained firmly behind it. Some of them had been with Fiorina throughout the merger process; others had joined HP from the Compaq board after the merger. They had, in Platt's words, "been through hell together." A united sense of purpose had been forged. "We were an iron stomach board with Carly," said Dunn.

"The outside perception is that the merger was a screw up, that it nearly wrecked the company. But that was absolutely wrong," said one director. "God knows where HP would be if we hadn't made the acquisition." Moreover, the execution of the merger had been by all accounts extraordinarily successful. Fiorina's team had achieved huge cost savings, and had done so right on schedule.

No, the problem the board had with Carly Fiorina had nothing to do with the merger, and little to do with the company's strategy. It was much more personal. It had to do with her and her management style.

Throughout 2004, concerns on the board about Fiorina's management had been growing. The company that David Packard and William Hewlett had built was a decentralized collection of individual businesses, in which each unit head had end-to-end responsibility. At the time Fiorina took over, there were at least 60 different businesses. Fiorina, under the board's direction, had taken that company and centralized it under her control, creating a matrix management structure designed to pull the units together.

The result, however, was a structure that was so complex and multilayered the board could no longer understand it. When things went wrong, there was no one to take responsibility, no one clearly to blame. The only person with unambiguous authority was Fiorina herself. And she was on the road so often—giving as many as 130 speeches her final year in office—that disputes remained unresolved and decisions unmade.

"We were hopelessly confounded by the organizational structure, and didn't have confidence it could succeed," Dunn told me later. Another director said: "The big issue was the depth of operating management. The company just didn't have enough of that."

The abrupt firings by Fiorina after the third quarter miss had only increased the directors' discomfort. Instead of taking the blame, Fiorina laid it harshly on those beneath her. In a brutal, finger-pointing conference call at the time, Fiorina told the soon-to-be-banished executives: "You've let H-P down, you've let the board down and you've let me down."

The board was also feeling pressures of its own. In the wake of the corporate scandals of 2001 and 2002, new standards were being set for boards of directors. They were being held accountable—by shareholders, by regulators, by trial lawyers—for the performance and the behavior of the companies on whose boards they sat.

Some of the changes in the way boards were operating were required by the Sarbanes-Oxley law, passed by Congress in the wake of the corporate scandals. Some were embodied in new guidelines for directors adopted by the New York Stock Exchange and other exchanges. Some were demanded by activist shareholders, or as a response to lawsuits brought against directors at the scandal-ridden companies. Directors were being forced to wake up, to take respon-sibility, and to recognize that board membership wasn't just a cushy honor—it was a heavy responsibility.

They also began to meet more often in executive session, with-out the CEO present. In the old days, such meetings had been rare—and often a sure sign the CEO was in trouble. At HP, such ex-ecutive sessions became the rule shortly after Fiorina took charge.

Once in such sessions, the board became less clubby. The so-cial dynamics shifted. Even the most prominent, successful and strong-willed business leaders were often reluctant to state their minds in board meetings if the CEO was present. With the CEO gone, however, more candid—and more critical—conversations became common.

Another important change in board dynamics came from the increasing reluctance of CEOs to sit on the boards of other compa-nies. In the old days, this had been a common practice, creating a kind of you-scratch-my-back-I'll-scratch-yours environment. A popular CEO might well lend his expertise to a half-dozen other boards. And since the CEO didn't want to be challenged on his own turf, he was less likely to challenge other CEOs on theirs.

But as the demands on board members and the risks of board membership increased, sitting CEOs cut back their outside board memberships. They didn't have the time to devote to boards that were meeting more and more often, and they couldn't afford to risk getting caught up in some other company's scandals. Moreover, increasingly, CEOs found that their own directors didn't want them to sit on outside boards.

In January of 2005, there were no CEOs on the Hewlett-Packard board. Boeing CEO Phil Condit had been a member before his company got caught up in a Washington scandal, forcing him to leave. So had Sam Ginn, onetime chairman and chief executive of AirTouch Communications, which later merged with Vodafone. As head of the board's nominating committee, Ginn had tried to recruit Chevron Corporation's CEO David O'Reilly, on whose board he sat. But O'Reilly had declined because of time pressures, and Ginn had subsequently retired, leaving the HP board without a single CEO member.

The most powerful wake-up call for corporate boards arrived with earth-shaking suddenness on January 7, 2005—just three days before the three HP directors met with Fiorina. On that day, news broke that 10 former board members of WorldCom had agreed to pay investors $18 million *out of their own pockets* as part of the settlement in the giant accounting fraud case involving that company. And 10 former board members of Enron agreed to pay $13 million, also *out of their own pockets*.

This was something new in the corporate world. Directors had certainly been sued before for the misdeeds of corporations. But generally, the company had taken out insurance policies to cover such charges. In the case of Enron and WorldCom, directors were forced to make payments beyond the insurance payments. And big payments. The WorldCom directors faced penalties amounting to an extraordinary 20 percent of their entire net worth.

For directors everywhere, that was like a bucket of cold water poured over their heads. Board duty suddenly became not just a burdensome responsibility, but also a financial risk. Many people with significant net worth decided they could no longer afford the liability, and began stepping down from their boards. Others refused to sign up. How could they expose themselves to such losses? It wasn't fair to their families, to their heirs.

None of this was lost on members of the HP board. There was a new climate in the boardroom, and it was partly a climate of fear— fear that they might be held personally and financially responsible for the performance or misdeeds of the corporation; fear of public humiliation.

For HP, all those forces had come into play the previous November, during an executive session following the board's regular meeting. That's when the dissatisfaction with Fiorina's leadership began to come into focus. Among other things, board members felt they needed to boost their own expertise.

At the meeting, Keyworth started arguing that Tom Perkins be brought back on the board. Perkins was a boisterous Silicon Valley legend, in love with fast cars, large sailboats and getting his way. He had worked for HP in the 1950s and 1960s and had helped the company start its computer business. In 1972, he cofounded Kleiner Perkins Caufield & Byers, one of the first Silicon Valley venture capital firms that made billions for its partners and investors by bankrolling start-up companies like Genentech Inc. and Netscape Inc. He had been a director of Compaq when it merged with HP, and had served on the merged company's board until March of the previous year, when he hit the retirement age.

Moreover, Keyworth considered Perkins his closest friend. He had gone to visit him in England earlier that year, and had concluded that bringing Perkins back on the board was critical, because Perkins understood technology while many other board members—Dunn, for instance—did not.

■

When informed at the end of the session that the board wanted to bring back Perkins, Fiorina balked. "I don't think lack of technical expertise is our biggest problem on this board," she said. "I think operational and big-company experience is a far greater need." She also questioned how it would look to bring back a board member who had passed the mandatory retirement age.

Besides, she added. "Do we even know whether he's interested?"

Keyworth jumped in. "As you know, Carly, I went to England to visit Tom on vacation. I think he really misses the board and would love to come back." Keyworth suggested inviting him to the January off-site board meeting so he could "get back up to speed."

Perkins had been a meddlesome director, creating the board's technology committee and frequently meeting with company employees. But Keyworth was persistent. Fiorina thought it odd at the time, but consented to having the venture capitalist join them at their January meeting.

Perkins says he later called Fiorina directly to find out if she supported his return to the board. "I didn't want to go on the board if the CEO wasn't totally enthusiastic," he said. Fiorina reassured him she was.

In retrospect, Perkins claims he didn't know at the time he agreed to rejoin the board about the directors' growing dissatisfaction with Fiorina. If he had, he says, he might not have signed up.

In any event, he found out soon enough. Though he still hadn't been formally elected to the board, he was invited to participate in a series of phone calls in December of 2004 and January of 2005—phone calls that involved most of the outside directors, but not Fiorina herself. They were highly unusual meetings—Fiorina would later argue, highly improper meetings—and it was in those meetings that the directors' complaints about Fiorina crystallized.

Some directors said they found it difficult to talk with Fiorina about their concerns. She didn't take well to criticism, they felt, and wasn't inclined to listen to their views. They decided they needed to send her a message, and deputized the three directors to do the job. In the days before the meeting, Dunn carefully negotiated the wording of a memo that stated the concerns on which all directors agreed.

It was that memo that Dunn held in her hands on January 10, as the three directors met with Fiorina. For the first 15 minutes or so of the meeting, the three directors stuck closely to that script.

First, they said, board members were concerned about their relationship with the CEO. She was not willing, they felt, to consider their input or advice. There was no real communication. A symptom of the problem: the board felt it had no involvement in setting the agenda for board meetings.

Second, directors felt the competitive position of the company's "enterprise" business—which served other companies—was not satisfactory. And they had no confidence that things would improve without major organizational changes.

Third, the board felt that Fiorina needed to take action to build her credibility in the financial markets, which had been roughed up during the merger battle and had been dented further by the third quarter miss. She needed to show some flexibility—a willingness to consider midcourse corrections. Many on Wall Street felt HP was hopelessly squeezed between Dell, the low-cost seller of computers, and IBM, the high-end provider of computer services. They wanted to see the company broken up, so individual units could more clearly focus on competing head-to-head with, say, Lexmark, the challenger in the printer business, or Dell in the computer business.

The board wasn't arguing for a breakup, like many Wall Street analysts were. And directors weren't asking Fiorina to step aside. Members of the board insist that on January 10, they had not yet imagined that they were on the road to her dismissal. "There was no thought that Carly wouldn't continue to be CEO," insists Perkins. But they did feel Fiorina needed to show some flexibility and make some changes.

Fiorina was clearly surprised by the statements. When she wanted, she had an extraordinary ability to project warmth and to charm the people in her presence. But she could also throw an arctic chill over them. Dunn, Hackborn and Keyworth—particularly Keyworth—had disturbed her with their insistence. Rather than turn on the charm, she froze them out.

Fiorina was a woman, after all, who had succeeded in a man's world. She had made it to the pinnacle of power, and had become her own boss. But now, these three directors were challenging that control. They were telling her how to manage her company. They were telling her how to do her job. Had anyone ever dared to have such conversations with her male predecessors at HP or Lucent or AT&T? This, she thought, was not the way the world was supposed to work. "I don't think that managing a company is a board's job," she said later. It was her job.

As the conversation continued, some of the board members got more specific. Keyworth, who headed the technology committee, began pushing for Fiorina to divide the company into two units, with a new president for each. He suggested that Shane Robison, the company's chief technology officer, be asked to head a combined Customer Solutions Group and Technology Solutions Group.

Vyomesh Joshi would become president of a combined Personal Systems Group and Imaging and Printing Group.

Fiorina recoiled at the specificity of the suggestions. Robison? In some ways, she thought, Keyworth and Robison were similar—introverted, a little geeky, loved technology but knew little about operating big organizations. Robison had never had responsibility over the profits and losses of a division. He certainly wasn't ready for such a big management job. What was Keyworth talking about? Choosing management—that was her job, not the board's.

Fiorina was also irritated by the charge that she wasn't open to board involvement. From where she sat, the board seemed very involved—sometimes, too involved. When Tom Perkins came on the board the first time around, he had suggested setting up a technology committee, and she had agreed. "The committee was very active in the company," Perkins acknowledged, "and she never objected." Fiorina also encouraged the board to meet regularly in executive session. She told the three directors that she was far more open to board involvement than other CEOs on whose boards she sat—citing Cisco CEO John Chambers as an example.

Still, it was clear to Fiorina that something unusual was happening. She didn't agree with much of what these directors were saying, and she wasn't sure it was their place to be saying it. But she saw they were serious, and she bowed to their first demand. She agreed to tear up the agenda for the off-site board meeting scheduled to begin that Wednesday night in San Francisco, and instead turn over the agenda to the issues they had raised.

It had been a tense meeting. Still, Dunn, Keyworth and Hackborn left feeling somewhat better. Fiorina hadn't conceded any of their points. She had, however, for the first time, in their view, engaged in a serious dialogue. She had allowed them to do the job they felt they had to do as directors in the new corporate world.

The San Francisco board meeting began with a dinner on

Wednesday night. Keyworth brought his new girlfriend, and proudly introduced her to the crowd. As Fiorina recalls it, Keyworth also made an effort that Wednesday night to get her to agree to put Tom Perkins on the board immediately. She argued that it wasn't appropriate to formally add him to the board until the annual meeting. Weeks later, in trying to understand how the board had turned against her so quickly, Fiorina remembered Keyworth's insistence. Was his effort to get Perkins on board part of a plan to unseat her?

The next day, Fiorina opened the meeting by asking each board member to make comments. The result was something less than unity. They had lots of ideas for improving the company, but it wasn't clear to Fiorina there was a consensus. They talked about different structures, and different people, with no agreement emerging.

Fiorina tried to convince the board members that the differences among them were not that great. She unveiled a plan to give Vyomesh Joshi—known inside as "VJ"—more day-to-day control of HP's printer and personal computer business—portraying it as a move in the direction of delegation that the board wanted. Many board members, however, thought combining the giant printing and personal computing businesses was a mistake. Meanwhile, Fiorina continued to stoutly resist putting Shane Robison into a major management job. She did indicate a willingness to consider bringing in new talent to take on a top management role in the months ahead. She just didn't want to do it right now. Their disagreements, she argued, were less about structure, more about people and timing.

Fiorina made another argument, which to her was the crux of the matter, and which she would restate repeatedly in the coming days of crisis. They had made her CEO, she told them. They held her accountable for the performance of the company. How could she be accountable if she couldn't choose her own management team?

After a day's worth of discussion, Fiorina made a suggestion. "It seems to me you have very different views of the key players," she said. "I think highly of Ann [Livermore], Jay, you don't. Some of you think highly of Shane. I think he's good, but not at an operating level. Bob Ryan is concerned about V.J. Why don't we have Shane & Ann & V.J. come in and spend an hour with you."

The meetings were arranged for Saturday, and the board spent an hour questioning the three. No decisions were made, but the meeting ended on a positive note. While little had been decided and Fiorina had remained largely unbending—"She redefined stone wall," Perkins said later—several directors nonetheless felt it had been the most candid and useful exchange they had ever had with her. For the first time, they thought, she had listened to their concerns.

"It was like the Berlin Wall had come down," Pattie Dunn told me later. "She was straining to try and get a coherent message from the board. She expressed some frustration and disagreement. She was more candid and expressed more frank assessments of people than she had in the past. It was like making a sausage. But at the end, the mood was cautiously optimistic." The board was hopeful "that she was starting to see why it made more sense to create clear lines of sight . . . and have more empowered executives. But we also agreed she would figure out how to make it happen. She would figure out the details."

That Saturday night, the group attended a party for a retiring HP executive, and Fiorina remembers a spirit of congeniality. She sat with Jay Keyworth and his girlfriend and Pattie Dunn and her husband. She recalls Hackborn telling her she "did the right thing." She recalls Keyworth making a good-natured suggestion that the next meeting be held aboard her yacht. Pattie Dunn's husband talked about their upcoming trip to Indonesia, and jokingly suggested Fiorina should retire so she and her husband could go with them on the trip. Pattie interrupted, saying that for her to encourage Fiorina to retire would be a "breach of my fiduciary duty."

The board and the chief executive, all thought, had begun to forge a new relationship. No one seemed to have an inkling of what was to come. Indeed, just a couple weeks later, when Fiorina was waiting in a hotel room to hear the verdict of her board, her husband comforted her by reminding her of the pleasant evening they had spent with the board that Saturday in San Francisco. How could these people, who clearly held her in high esteem, fire her?

6

Hank Greenberg had encountered many politicians and government officials during his long years atop the insurance giant AIG. But he had never encountered one like New York attorney general Eliot Spitzer. That became clear on October 14, 2004.

Spitzer was investigating the insurance industry, and had come across a practice by the big brokerage firms that sold insurance to companies that looked suspiciously like bid rigging. The attorney general's staff, which had been poring over files they had requested from the large insurance brokers, found an e-mail in September from a Marsh & McLennan broker to the insurance firm CNA, which asked the firm to make a bid "that is reasonably competitive but will not be a winner." This appeared to be a smoking gun—evidence of the company soliciting a false bid, apparently to make the bidding process look more competitive.

The attorney general's office sent out a quick subpoena to all brokers and insurance companies, asking them to submit within the next two weeks any information they had on "fictitious bids" or any "bid that was based on anything other than honest under-writing." This had become standard Spitzer operating procedure: blast companies with subpoenas that, in effect, forced them to do his leg work.

What happened next must have been the source of some tense conversations around the Greenberg family dinner table. Marsh & McLennan was headed by Hank Greenberg's oldest son, Jeffrey. But among the first insurance companies to offer damning evidence on Marsh's bid-rigging practices were AIG, headed by Jeffrey's father, and ACE, headed by his brother Evan. AIG, it turned out, was one of the biggest beneficiaries of Marsh's practices. When-ever an AIG customer's policy was up for renewal, Marsh brokers would call the company and suggest a premium. Then it would get other firms to provide higher bids, creating a false sense of compe-tition.

Armed with this information from father and brother, Spitzer went after Jeffrey Greenberg, and Marsh & McLennan. Not sensing the level of danger, the company stonewalled, insisting that Spitzer didn't understand how the insurance business worked. Impatient as always, Spitzer decided to go public.

In an extraordinary press conference on October 14, the attor-ney general accused the company of "classic cartel behavior," "col-lusion" and "price fixing." Then, warming to the moment, he angrily declared that the company's leadership "is not a leadership I will talk with. It is not a leadership I will negotiate with."

This was a stunning public statement from an attorney gen-eral. Spitzer had never talked to Jeffrey Greenberg, only to his at-torneys. It wasn't entirely clear that the younger Greenberg had ordered or even condoned his lawyers' stiff-armed behavior. And there was no evidence linking Greenberg to the bid-rigging. Nev-ertheless, Spitzer was convinced that the problems at Marsh &

McLennan started at the top. So he issued his statement, which could not have been clearer: Dump Jeffrey Greenberg, or you face the threat of indictment.

The immediate effect on Wall Street was stunning—Marsh & McLennan's stock dropped 25 percent. And the ramifications went much further than that. This was an unprecedented prosecutorial tactic. Big public companies like Marsh & McLennan couldn't afford to fight law enforcement authorities like Spitzer in court. The damage to their reputations that would result would destroy the business.

Anyone who doubted that only needed to look at what had happened to the accounting firm of Arthur Andersen. The accounting firm had been central to the scandal at Enron, providing advice on the transactions later found to be fraudulent. Moreover, when the investigation of Enron got under way, Andersen employees in the Houston office had engaged in a frenzy of document destruction. As a result, the Department of Justice had indicted not just the wrongdoers in Houston, but the entire firm—forcing it to surrender its licenses to practice accounting. The fact that in 2005 the Supreme Court overturned the government's conviction of Arthur Andersen was cold comfort. That decision came years too late to do the dismantled firm any good.

Spitzer, of course, knew exactly what he was doing. Appearing on CNBC's *Kudlow and Cramer* show, Spitzer was asked by his old school chum Cramer whether he was trying to put Marsh out of business.

"I'm not in the business of establishing ultimatums," Spitzer replied.

But could the company handle a felony charge, Cramer asked, if Spitzer brought one? Wouldn't it be put out of business?

"They might be," the prosecutor replied. "We'll have to see how this plays out. . . . And that is why, quite frankly, I was unhappy not to see something more fulsome from Marsh-Mac over the many months we've been having conversations with them."

Jeffrey Greenberg, who had inherited his father's pugnacious spirit, initially wanted to fight back. He scheduled a press conference to reply to the attorney general's allegations. He wanted to point out that he had never even talked to Spitzer about bid-rigging—why had he become the target? But his attorney, Richard Beattie, advised against it. The press conference was canceled. Instead, he did the only thing he could do under the circumstances—sent a letter to his board, offering to resign.

A Marsh board member, former U.S. attorney Zachary Carter, who had been put on the Marsh & McLennan board as a result of an earlier scandal, led a small group of independent directors to meet with Spitzer on Wednesday, October 20. They wanted to know if they really had to get rid of Greenberg. Spitzer was unyielding.

By the next weekend, Jeffrey Greenberg was out. And in a clear sign that board members understood who was really running the show, they appointed Michael Cherkasky, a former Spitzer colleague who was a top executive at Marsh, to replace him. Cherkasky announced the company would no longer accept commissions from the insurers it steered business to, and Spitzer announced criminal prosecution was no longer necessary.

Nothing like this had ever happened before in the business world. It was one thing for a state attorney general to prosecute a company or a top executive for a crime. But it was something else entirely to publicly demand—and get—a change in the company's leadership without any evidence of involvement in a crime. This had become Spitzer's standard method of operating. He used the media skillfully to put pressure on large public companies, and force them to settle. His courtroom was the press, and his jury, the general public. Even people in the business community who had been sympathetic to many of Spitzer's previous initiatives thought he had gone over the top this time. His job was to prosecute crimes in court, not to use bullying tactics to choose companies' CEOs.

Still, in the broader public debate, criticism of Spitzer's tactics remained muted. The editorial page of the *Wall Street Journal* blasted him, but most of the press remained friendly. Spitzer was an aggressive prosecutor, but more than that, he was a good politician. He knew that public sentiment was with him. The sour public opinion of business that had followed the stock market collapse and the corporate scandals earlier in the decade gave him the opening to make an unprecedented grab for power.

In his speeches, Spitzer sometimes compared himself with Teddy Roosevelt, who railed against business in the early years of the previous century. "We are heirs to one of the most august, powerful political traditions in the world—New York's proud progressive tradition, embodied by Teddy Roosevelt, Al Smith and FDR," he said. "Their example inspired me."

In a few short years, Spitzer had remade the investment banking industry, attacking the independence of stock analysis and the methods used for allocating initial public offerings. He had taken on the insurance industry and the mutual fund industry, and done battle with the former head of the New York Stock Exchange, Dick Grasso, over Grasso's excessive compensation.

Moreover, Spitzer's influence spread far beyond the cases that his hardworking prosecutors were pursuing. SEC and Justice Department officials didn't like to admit it, but he had humiliated them by taking the lead in investigating securities matters in their domain. In doing so, he had spurred them to become a far more aggressive regulatory and investigative force than anyone had ever expected them to be—particularly at a time when Republicans, members of the party of business, controlled the White House and both houses of Congress.

The combination of respect and jurisdictional resentment that Spitzer generated among regulators could be seen in a humorous but pointed speech Stephen Cutler of the SEC gave to the SEC Historical Society in 2003. In the speech, Cutler read from a series of fictional e-mails, such as one "from Eliot to the Vatican."

> *Dear Pontiff: I have some comments on recent papal edicts. While you are and should be the primary regulator of Catholicism, I believe you may be asleep at the switch on this whole business of transubstantiation. As I read the Stamp Act of 1785, I have the authority to tax and regulate all items passing through New York, which we believe includes Catholicism.*

Another e-mail was "from Eliot to heaven."

> *Dear God: It's my understanding that you are everywhere . . . including, apparently, the State of New York. As I read the Stamp Act of 1785, you are subject to regulation and taxation by the State of New York. While you are and should be the primary regulator of humanity, I have some ideas I'd like to share with you.*

Spitzer had also set an example for attorneys general in other states around the country. Like him, many AGs had higher political aspirations. He had demonstrated that attacking powerful corporations—once seen as a good way to kill a promising political career—was in fact a path to power. Business groups began talking about the frightening prospect of "fifty Spitzers."

The ousting of his son Jeffrey had a profound effect on Hank Greenberg. Spitzer was a regulator who was playing a different kind of power game. In Greenberg's world, up to that time, money—and particularly his money—had always prevailed. Indeed, he had made political contributions to Spitzer, as he had to many other powerful politicians on both sides of the political isle. But now he faced a politically ambitious attorney general who didn't care about all his contacts and all his money. Spitzer was determined to show the Greenberg family who was boss.

On October 25, as Jeffrey Greenberg was still negotiating final details of his departure from Marsh & McLennan, Hank Greenberg changed course. AIG released a two-sentence statement saying that it had instructed "its counsel to resolve" the outstanding regulatory issues "by reaching a prompt settlement in terms satisfactory" to AIG.

AIG brought in new outside counsel, led by Mark Pomerantz of the firm Paul, Weiss, Rifkind, Wharton & Garrison. By November, AIG had reached a settlement with the Justice Department and the Securities and Exchange Commission by which it agreed to pay $126 million in penalties and restitution for its transactions with Brightpoint and PNC Financial Sponsors. It also agreed to an independent monitor with even broader powers than the one in the settlement Greenberg had rejected just four months earlier.

Hank Greenberg, however, remained personally unrepentant.

In January of 2005, I was granted an audience with Greenberg. We were to have lunch together in his dining room on the top floor of the AIG building in lower Manhattan, overlooking New York Harbor. I was ushered into the reception room, where he greeted the world leaders of politics and business who regularly came to call on him, surrounded by the beautiful artifacts of past Asian empires.

His public relations advisers had agreed to arrange a meeting on one condition: that I not bring up the investigations against Greenberg and his company by Eliot Spitzer and the SEC. It would be inappropriate, they said, for him to talk about the investigations while they were still active.

I didn't bring up the investigations, but I didn't have to. After a brief, and tense, conversation about business in China, he couldn't restrain himself. He was angry, in part at my newspaper, for printing new details of Spitzer's campaign. Was it really fair, he asked, for the paper to let an overambitious attorney general promote his agenda by giving information to the *Wall Street Journal*? Shouldn't we be questioning Spitzer's tactics? Where was due process? Innocent until proven guilty?

Yet for all his anger, at that moment, Hank Greenberg still found it inconceivable that he could be kicked out of his job. He had built AIG from nothing. It wouldn't—couldn't—exist without him. He *was* AIG.

7

Less than a week after the HP board's meeting in San Francisco, director Lucille Salhany called Robert Sherbin, who ran corporate communications at HP. "We have a problem," she said. She had gotten a call from Pui-Wing Tam at the *Wall Street Journal*, who had complete details of the reorganization discussions that occurred at the board meeting, as well as all the details of the board's disagreements with Carly. The *Journal* was preparing to run a front-page story.

Sherbin called Fiorina, who was in Washington for the second inauguration of George W. Bush. Fiorina reacted with horror. The board was going to war with her in the press, she thought. This was outrageous—indeed, virtually unheard of in corporate America.

She felt violated. "When confidential board conversations become public," she said later, "then a very important bond of trust has been broken."

Fiorina sent an e-mail to board members and called for a telephone conference that weekend—even before the article appeared in the paper. During the call, she let loose her wrath. This was beyond the pale, she said. It was unforgiveable. "She was absolutely livid," recalls Tom Perkins.

Everyone agreed that the leak was a reprehensible breach of confidentiality. For boards to operate effectively, they all believed, they had to be able to have candid discussions in private. The *Wall Street Journal* story suggested that this was no longer the case. Yet no one confessed to the leak.

Someone asked whether it was possible that the room in San Francisco had been bugged. Fiorina assured them that she had swept it for bugs before the meeting, as was her usual practice. Lawrence Babbio, the Verizon executive who was one of Fiorina's closest allies on the board, even went so far as to suggest all the board members resign, and let Fiorina decide who should come back on.

But some of the directors also seemed to feel that Fiorina's highhanded lecture went too far. Sure, a trust had been broken. But not all the members of the board had broken it. And the directors still had a job to do. The fact that someone had leaked the story to the press didn't change the position of the company or its need, in their view, for management changes.

"Carly wanted to make the leaks the number one issue," Dunn said afterward. "The board was seeking to make performance the number one issue." Another board member gave a similar assessment. Carly "wanted to attack what to me was the lesser of two issues: the leak."

Whether a calculated move or a sincere emotional outburst—or some of both—Fiorina's response to the leak changed everything.

It's not clear that anyone realized it or articulated it at that moment, but the gulf between her and her board had become immense. They were on different islands, different continents, different planets—with completely differing views of their respective roles. They were operating with different rule books. And it was unlikely either side would try to bridge the gap.

Pui-Wing Tam's front-page story about the Hewlett-Packard board's disagreements with Carly Fiorina appeared in the paper on January 24. It was an extraordinary piece of journalism. Boards of directors certainly had tangled with chief executives in the past. But word of those struggles seldom leaked to the press—at least, until *after* the executive had resigned or been fired. Here was a case of the board airing its laundry right in the middle of the battle. Part of the story read:

> *Directors of Hewlett-Packard Co., unhappy with the uneven performance of the giant printer and computer maker, are considering a management reorganization that would distribute some key day-to-day responsibilities of Chairman and Chief Executive Carly Fiorina among other executives, said people familiar with the situation.*

The *directors* were considering a *management* reorganization? Over the *chief executive's* objection? That flew in the face of the entire American tradition of corporate management. At most, directors set strategy, served as a sounding board, and stepped in when things were seriously amiss. But seldom did they have either the time or the intention to actually try to dictate how the company should be run. Something big was afoot.

> *Ms. Fiorina "has tremendous abilities," one person close to the situation said. "But she shouldn't be running every-*

thing every day. She is very hands on, and that slows things down."

In the third paragraph, though, was the sentence that caught my attention: "Ms. Fiorina, who plans to attend the World Economic Forum in Davos, Switzerland, declined through an H-P spokesman to comment."

I'd attended the World Economic Forum on a number of occasions over the previous decade, and I knew its attractions. For one thing, it happens in one of the most beautiful villages in Europe, nestled peacefully in the snow-covered Swiss Alps (with excellent skiing). And it brings together a rare collection of the leaders of business, government, nonprofit groups and the arts. It's the place where you find Bill Gates and Nelson Mandela rubbing elbows, or find Bill Clinton up all night in serious discussions with Angelina Jolie and Richard Gere. It was the ultimate networking opportunity for the world's power elite—so much so that it had become a top target for antiglobalization protestors in recent years, and had to be protected with fortresslike barricades and imposing water canons. For a woman like Carly Fiorina, enjoying her position of prominence, it was an intoxicating environment.

Yet it was not the place for a CEO to be when her job was on the line. Her board was pushing for a major reorganization of the company over her objections . . . and she was going to Davos? I checked the schedule and found she was slated to appear on a panel whose topic of discussion was entitled "Does Business Have a Noble Purpose?"—an odd topic for a woman about to lose her business.

I made it my mission to find Fiorina in Davos. I attended the "Noble Purpose" session, only to learn that she had canceled, because of a scheduling conflict. I called her press assistant, and was told she planned to have a small coffee klatch with reporters at the

Hotel Rinaldi later that day. I was told the session was full, but managed to maneuver my way into it.

At the coffee klatch, I asked Fiorina why she had come to Davos, and whether that was the best use of her time, given HP's challenges. "I get the opportunity to meet with a huge number of customers," she replied, citing as an example her breakfast that morning with Tony Blair, the prime minister of Great Britain. When I asked what she thought of the story in the *Wall Street Journal* earlier that week, she gave an answer along the lines of "Don't believe everything you read in the press."

So I tried it another way: "How would *you* describe your relations with the board?" She replied, "Excellent."

Perhaps, at that moment, Fiorina believed that her relations with the board were excellent—or at least, good enough. The leak had at least given her the sense she occupied the moral high ground. She had brought in attorney Larry Sonsini to investigate, and he was methodically talking to each of the board members, and reporting back to her.

In an interview with Sonsini, Tom Perkins had admitted to talking with Pui-Wing Tam, but said he did so only after receiving an e-mail that made it clear she had the story. He just wanted to make sure she had it right, he said. If Perkins was the second source, however, who was the first? No one confessed.

On Friday, January 28, the board held another phone conference and heard Sonsini's report. There were more recriminations, but no conclusions. Fiorina suspected Keyworth, but he kept quiet. Meanwhile, board members were growing frustrated because Fiorina insisted on focusing only on the leak—not on their concerns about the company's management structure. All agreed that they needed to hold another meeting to clear the air, and decided they would gather on February 7 at a place to be determined later.

Pattie Dunn, who had left with her husband for their vacation in

Java immediately after the San Franciso meeting, had missed out on all the board fireworks. She was out of touch, and knew nothing of the leak, or Fiorina's reaction to it, until she arrived at the airport in Hong Kong on January 31, and checked her e-mail. It was clear to her that all the progress made in San Francisco had been erased.

On Wednesday, February 2, Dunn was having lunch with a friend at the Lark Creek Inn in Larkspur, California, talking about her Java experiences, when her cell phone rang. It was Fiorina. In all the years Dunn had been on the HP board, she couldn't remember the CEO ever calling her before. "She had a reputation among directors for often not being responsive to their calls and emails," Dunn said.

Dunn walked out onto a patio to take the call. Fiorina asked about the logistical details of the meeting on the following Monday—Dunn had arranged for it to happen in Chicago, at the airport Hyatt hotel, because that seemed the easiest place for all directors to reach.

Then Fiorina asked Dunn, "Is there anything I should be thinking about" to prepare for the meeting.

"I told her I felt the setback and her reaction to the leaks had put us back to a point that had seemingly undone the positive progress at the offsite. If she could tell the board she was looking to put that whole experience to the side and work on the business issues we talked about, then I believed the board continued to want to see her succeed."

What Dunn didn't tell her was that on Sunday night, the directors were having dinner without Fiorina with attorney Larry Sonsini and with John Coffee, a Columbia Law School professor and expert on corporate governance. Coffee's presence was a clear sign the board was preparing to take the most drastic action a board can take—dismissing the CEO. Directors wanted to make sure they were on solid ground in making the move.

Fiorina spent that Sunday with her husband, Frank, suspicious that something was afoot. She was particularly disturbed by the re-emergence of Tom Perkins and his role in the board's maneuverings. Her husband tried to calm her, and told her to stop worrying. While she had been slow to recognize the board's concerns, she now knew something was out of kilter.

She arrived at the Hyatt Regency O'Hare in Chicago on Monday morning, with a letter, of four or five pages, that she intended to read to the board. She recalls noticing Keyworth whispering in Dunn's ear as the meeting started.

According to minutes of that meeting, Bob Knowling opened the session and called for the first order of business, which was for the board to accept the resignation of Disney executive Sandy Litvack—who told the board he would rather resign than be a part of whatever was going to happen at the meeting. Then Pattie Dunn was elected presiding director.

Dunn asked the board to vote on Tom Perkins's reelection. Fiorina abstained. Two others voted no—it was the first time in Fiorina's memory that a board decision was less than unanimous.

Dunn then said, "Carly, do you have anything to say?" Fiorina passed around copies of her statement, and read through it, uninterrupted.

"I serve at the pleasure of the Board," she began. "I have served in order to build a great company." She detailed her agreements and differences with the board on executing the company's strategy, on individual managers, and on board communications. The memo was her attempt to address the board's concerns. But Pattie Dunn said the implicit message behind it was "I'm CEO, and you are not."

When Fiorina finally finished reading, she waited for questions. There were none.

Instead, she was asked to leave the room.

For the next three hours, she sat in her hotel room with her husband. It gradually began to dawn on her what was happening. Her husband tried to reassure her. "It's impossible," he said. "They wouldn't do that."

Finally, Larry Sonsini called her and asked her to come downstairs. Most of the board members had left—only Pattie Dunn, Bob Knowling and Larry Sonsini were still there. Knowling said, "The board has decided to make a change. I'm very sorry." Knowling, along with Babbio, had voted against her ouster. Dunn, suddenly the board's chairman, moved quickly to the mechanics, saying they wanted to make an announcement immediately, and said the board thought Fiorina should announce it as her own decision.

Shocked, Fiorina said she needed to think about it. "You have been thinking about this; I haven't." From her plane on the ride home, however, she had Larry Sonsini call back with her response. She wasn't going to resign. Instead, she began to write out the statement that would be released the next day:

> *While I regret the board and I have differences about how to execute HP's strategy, I respect their decision.*

In the months that followed, Fiorina wondered at the abruptness of it all. Certainly the board had the right to remove her as CEO. But did it need to happen so quickly, with so little warning and no transition? Could there have been a gradual handoff of power? That had been the way in other companies . . . a transition, a celebration of the departing CEO's contributions.

On CBS's *60 Minutes* a year and a half later, interviewer Lesley Stahl asked Fiorina if missing a quarter's earnings estimates by 20 percent and presiding over a tumbling stock price weren't reasons enough to dismiss her.

"Well, they could be," Fiorina replied. "But you would think, if those were the reasons, that after all this heavy lifting, and after all this work, at least the board would sit me down and say, 'You know, Carly, we think, unfortunately, that it's time to make a move because dot, dot, dot. Let's talk about these things.' That conversation didn't happen.

"After I was fired, they put the CFO in charge. They paid him $3.5 million for 45 days' worth of work, and then they hired my successor in apparently ten days. That's not a very well thought-through succession plan for an $85 billion company."

But in 2005, boards had lost their patience. The CEO was no longer invulnerable.

Frank Zarb was one person Hank Greenberg thought he could trust. The two men had known each other for 20 years, since financier Felix Rohatyn had introduced them in the 1980s. They had worked together on several business deals. On a couple of occasions, they had enjoyed social dinners together, or gone to the theater with their wives. Greenberg was a man who knew everyone, but had few real friends. Zarb was as close as he got.

Greenberg liked to take credit for at least one of Zarb's career successes. In 1994, the search firm of Spencer Stuart approached Zarb about a job as chief executive of Alexander and Alexander Services Inc., a global insurance brokerage firm. Zarb was interested, but felt the firm lacked sufficient capital, and didn't want to join an undercapitalized firm. Separately, Greenberg had been talking to Alexander and Alexander about its problems, and was considering making an investment. His one demand: find a good CEO.

When Greenberg learned that Zarb might get the job, he made it clear: hire Zarb and he'd put in $250 million.

In retrospect, Greenberg saw that as the moment when he gave Frank Zarb what he most wanted: an opportunity to run his own company. Zarb, however, is quick to recall that two and a half years later, when he sold the firm, he returned $360 million to Greenberg, giving him a very nice return on his investment. The obligation was repaid. In any case, it was a bond that was forever broken by the tumultuous events of 2005.

Frank Zarb was born to immigrant parents in Brooklyn, New York, and never imagined growing up that he would reach the top ranks of American business. His father was a refrigerator repair man. Frank went to the Manhattan High School of Aviation Trades, figuring he would become an airline mechanic.

An English teacher in high school saw his talent, however, took an interest in him, and eventually helped him get into Hofstra University.

After a stint in the military, Zarb went to work for Cities Service Oil Company, to run its training programs. His debut on Wall Street came in 1962, when he was hired by a securities firm, Goodbody and Company, to run the back-office operation. He later joined up with Sandy Weill, future CEO of Citigroup, and Arthur Levitt, future chairman of the SEC, as they built up the investment banking business that eventually became Lehman Brothers. Weill and Levitt were the front men for the business. Zarb was always, as he put it, "the back-office man."

His reputation as a manager brought Zarb to the attention of aides of President Richard Nixon, who had made it a goal to put good managers into government. At Nixon's call, Zarb left New York to become assistant secretary for management at the Department of Labor.

His performance in Washington was good enough to get him a job offer to help run President Nixon's reelection effort in 1972—CREEP, or the Committee to Reelect the President. Fortunately for him, he declined the job and returned to New York—leaving the position instead to a young man named Jeb Magruder, who ultimately pleaded guilty to planning the events leading to the Watergate break-in.

Zarb returned to Washington during the second Nixon administration, taking a job at the Office of Management and Budget. He stayed on after Nixon resigned in 1974, and in the wake of the oil crisis, became the nation's "Energy Czar." Then he returned to Wall Street in 1977, to work at the investment banking firm of Lazard Freres. It was there that he first met and worked with Greenberg. He reunited with his former partner Sandy Weill in 1988 at Travelers Inc., worked his way up to become chief executive of Travelers subsidiary Smith Barney, before leaving in 1994 to head Alexander and Alexander.

With a mixture of government and Wall Street background, Zarb had the perfect resume for his next job—chief executive of the National Association of Securities Dealers, which runs the NASDAQ, a position he held until 2001, riding the technology stock boom that took the NASDAQ market to extraordinary highs before bringing it crashing back down to earth.

When he left the NASD in 2001, the Enron scandal hadn't yet hit. And while big companies felt some pressure to hire "independent" directors to sit on their boards, those boards remained fairly clubby affairs. Greenberg liked having former government officials on his board, he trusted Zarb, and so he asked him to join. Shortly thereafter, when it became clear the board needed a lead director, Greenberg asked Zarb to take on the task.

The most important job of any board of directors is planning the succession of the CEO. With Greenberg approaching 80 years of age, this was certainly an issue worthy of attention at AIG. In his role as lead director, Zarb would occasionally discuss the issue with Greenberg, during their monthly lunches of scrod and vegetables—the AIG chief's unvarying diet. In response, the CEO would read Zarb a secret letter that he kept hidden in his office, outlining who should take control of the company if something were to happen to him. He had identified two AIG employees—Martin Sullivan and Donald Kanak—as the most qualified to take his place. Over time, it became clear that Sullivan was his favorite. But Greenberg had no interest in letting other people know about the contents of that letter, and no plans to step down anytime soon. AIG was his life.

The AIG board had always let Greenberg have his way on most big issues, primarily because on most big issues, he had so often been right. One board member told me being an AIG director was one of the easiest jobs around, because Hank did such a good job running the company. The directors, for the most part, didn't have to worry.

But as the SEC and Eliot Spitzer began nosing into AIG's business, the board grew increasingly uncomfortable. Greenberg's take-no-prisoners approach worried them, in part because it seemed so counterproductive. His stonewalling had only made the regulators more angry. His refusal to settle with the SEC in August seemed especially foolish. He had been forced to settle a few weeks later at a much higher cost.

Moreover, AIG directors—like others across the country—realized they had to view their responsibilities in a new light. They worked for the shareholders, not for Hank. As the suits against directors of Enron and WorldCom demonstrated, if anything went wrong, they could be held personally liable.

By the beginning of 2005, the board had come to the conclusion that something had to change at AIG. To those like Zarb, who had spent time in Washington, Greenberg's eagerness to do battle with regulators seemed increasingly unwise. The ultimate danger was the possibility that the Justice Department or Spitzer might indict AIG. For most people, an indictment is the beginning of the legal process. For a big public company that trades upon its reputation, an indictment is a death sentence.

Recognizing the problem, Zarb and a handful of his fellow board members began to plot ways to ease Greenberg out of his job. It was time for him to retire. The recent indications of bad judgment, they thought, might be the result of old age.

For help, Zarb turned to Dick Beattie of the law firm Simpson Thatcher—an experienced veteran of corporate battles, who, ironically, also had represented Jeffrey Greenberg in the Marsh & McLennan affair. Greenberg was furious when he heard about it—why did the board need its own counsel, he asked? Weren't AIG's own lawyers sufficient? It was the opening of a gulf between Zarb and Greenberg that would only grow wider in the coming weeks.

With Beattie's help, the board arranged a discussion with Greenberg at a dinner during the January board meeting. With no other company managers present, several directors expressed their belief that it was time for him to prepare for retirement. Greenberg appeared to concede, saying he was ready to announce plans to step down and that Martin Sullivan would be his successor. A press release was drawn up for release the next day.

The next morning, however, Greenberg once again pulled back. He called Zarb and said he had changed his mind. He'd be willing to announce Sullivan as his successor at the annual meeting in May. But he wasn't prepared to set a date for his retirement. Although he was almost 80, Greenberg wasn't ready to bow out.

Then on February 9—the same day that Hewlett-Packard was announcing the departure of Carly Fiorina—a bombshell hit. The company received a series of subpoenas focusing on a transaction it had engaged in with another insurance company, called General Reinsurance, or Gen Re, which was owned by Warren Buffett's Berkshire Hathaway. Unlike the complaints settled in November, which dealt with AIG's involvement in efforts to clean up other companies' books, this one appeared to be about AIG's efforts to clean up its own books. Greenberg's contention had always been that his company simply sold the insurance products, and shouldn't be held accountable if others misused them. But this time, it was AIG that appeared to be misusing those products.

It was a serious escalation in the prosecutor's battle with the company. AIG's lawyers immediately dug in, to learn what they could about the transaction that had caught Spitzer's attention. The more they learned, the more disturbed they became.

For one thing, the transaction had been initiated by Greenberg himself. In late 2000, he had called Ronald Ferguson, then chief executive of Gen Re, to set up a sale of so-called "finite risk" insurance. The transaction was an arcane one, but it essentially allowed AIG to book $500 million in premium revenue in return for taking on "risks" also valued at $500 million. That enabled the company to add $500 million to its loss reserves, answering the criticism of some analysts that the company hadn't put enough money aside to cover losses.

The underlying question was whether AIG had actually taken on any risk in the transaction—in which case the $500 million could be booked as insurance premium—or whether Gen Re had in effect promised to offset any losses—in which case this was simply a loan, and shouldn't have been booked as insurance income. The latter seemed to be the case.

AIG brought in the team from Paul Weiss again, and the lawyers worked round the clock to learn what they could about the transaction. None of what they learned was very good. Particularly disturbing was the role of Christian Milton, whose job at AIG was to oversee the selling of reinsurance, not to be buying such insurance. Greenberg had apparently gotten him involved because of his close relationship with Gen Re. There were a series of e-mails from Milton that suggested this was a sham transaction, and that Milton was somehow trying to hide how the fees were flowing.

In the old days, this kind of transaction might have been typical of the cozy dealings between big insurance companies. Relationships mattered. These were gentlemen's deals in which one company helped another, and no one got hurt. But Spitzer didn't care about the old days. To him, this sort of dealing was designed to fool shareholders, and he wasn't going to tolerate it.

Not about to be outdone again by Spitzer, the SEC also jumped into the act. It sent its own subpoena to AIG. Greenberg responded in usual fashion, directly calling the SEC's Stephen Cutler. "I thought we settled" our differences, Greenberg said. Cutler explained this was an entirely new matter, involving not products AIG sold to other companies, but AIG's own books.

On February 14, AIG announced it had received the subpoenas. In short order, its stock price fell more than four dollars. Greenberg, who through his wife was the company's biggest shareholder, called his trading desk and ordered them to start purchasing stock, in an obvious effort to prop up the price. He called back several times, urging the traders to be more aggressive in their buying—actions that subsequently caused regulators to begin investigating whether he was guilty of improper stock manipulation.

Recognizing that the directors had a big problem on their hands, Zarb decided the time had come to act. With the board's backing, he seized control of the internal investigation, and told the lawyers from Paul Weiss to report directly to him. On February 25, the Paul

Weiss team met at the SEC's offices in New York City with Spitzer's lawyers, the SEC lawyers, and the AIG board lawyers. They laid out the facts on the Gen Re transaction, admitting it was "problematic."

Meanwhile, Spitzer's team was pushing to depose Greenberg himself. The company's lawyers kept trying to put it off, but the Attorney General's Office was insistent. Greenberg had hired feisty defense lawyer Robert Morvillo, who had represented domestic doyenne Martha Stewart in her trial, and he made it clear he thought the AIG chief should refuse to testify, claiming his Fifth Amendment right. That created even more pressure on the board, which had already adopted a policy indicating that AIG would cooperate with investigators. How could AIG say that it was cooperating if its chief executive was refusing to testify?

On March 12, Spitzer was preparing for a jog in Central Park when he got a call from Richard Beattie. Beattie wanted to know from Spitzer just how bad things were. The two met in the park, and Spitzer dropped a bombshell. Among other things, the attorney general had tapes, not with Hank Greenberg on them, but with other people discussing what Greenberg knew about the Gen Re deal, and what he wanted out of it. The tapes made it absolutely clear to Spitzer that the whole transaction was bogus.

This time, Spitzer didn't deliver an ultimatum. Beattie had previously told the attorney general that he had erred in demanding Jeffrey Greenberg's head in the Marsh & McLennan affair. So this time, Spitzer held off. But the message was still hard to escape.

Convinced the company had reached a moment of truth, Beattie and Zarb called a board meeting for Sunday, March 13. In a critical miscalculation, Greenberg, who'd been asked to attend the meeting and speak to the directors, chose not to. Instead, he stuck with his plans of going out on his yacht in Florida—the *Serendipity II*, owned by an AIG-related company, also headed by Greenberg. He was angry about the board's hiring of Beattie, angry about the board's takeover of the investigation, and angry that they were meeting to discuss his fate.

The directors met in the midtown offices of Beattie's law firm, Simpson Thatcher. Zarb began by making it clear that the directors' job was to represent shareholders, not Hank Greenberg. He tried to let the conversation take its own course. But it wasn't long before most of the directors came to the same conclusion Zarb had already reached.

At the meeting, the Paul Weiss lawyers told what they knew about the Gen Re deal, which was disturbing enough. Beattie reported what he had learned from Spitzer in Central Park the previous day.

Perhaps most disturbing was the presence of Barry Winograd, who handled AIG's account with the firm Price Waterhouse Coopers. In one of the great ironies of the accounting scandals of 2001 and 2002, accountants—who had been at the heart of the scandals—had emerged with much greater power. Under the Sarbanes-Oxley law, they had to sign off on a company's annual filings, known as 10-Ks, and had to certify that there was a tone at the top of the company conducive to accurate accounting. AIG's 10-K was due in just a few days.

The directors asked Winograd whether he'd be willing to sign the company's 10-K with Greenberg still the CEO. Winograd danced around the issue, but wouldn't say yes. That left the directors with the clear impression that the answer was no.

While Spitzer wasn't demanding Hank Greenberg's resignation, the company's auditors, in effect, were. In the post-Enron environment, the accountants were a major power that couldn't be ignored.

The meeting dragged on for 10 hours. Greenberg called in from time to time from the boat, and later from the AIG corporate jet. As he sensed the direction of the meeting, he grew angry and abusive.

The board, he complained, was being led around by the nose by a bunch of lawyers "who couldn't even spell insurance."

Carla Hills, the former U.S. trade negotiator, defended the CEO. But one by one, the other board members came to the conclusion that he couldn't stay. As the day wore on, they decided he should step down immediately as CEO, but stay on as chairman. Zarb and Beattie informed him of the decision that night.

Needless to say, Greenberg wasn't happy. On Monday morning, he walked into an office where his top lieutenants were preparing for the announcement that he was stepping down. "Are you ready?" Martin Sullivan asked him. "Ready as I'll ever be," Greenberg grumbled.

Then he turned to his general counsel, Ernie Patrikis, and pointed at him. "You are the cause of this," he said. "You are the one who brought in the outside lawyers." He added, threateningly, "One day, some people who work here won't be working here any more."

It was a painful moment for all. Greenberg's lieutenants were unfailingly loyal to him. He was their lodestar, and he had made them all rich. But now, they could tell, he felt betrayed by them. He felt especially betrayed by Zarb.

The next evening, the board held a dinner that Greenberg attended. He sat through most of the meal silently, with his arms crossed. Finally, Bernard Aidinoff, a board member and friend for 40 years, stood up to offer a toast "to a great, great friend" and to the man who made "AIG the great company it is today." Everyone else stood up and toasted. Greenberg didn't respond.

There was a long silence. Then he said, "Let's go home now."

The directors held their regular meeting the next day, and it quickly became clear to Hank Zarb that they still hadn't gone far enough. As long as Greenberg was chairman, it seemed, the auditors would have problems signing the company's 10-K. Moreover, it was far from clear that Greenberg was really ready to let Martin Sullivan run the company unimpeded.

Hearing the rumblings, Greenberg appealed to powerful friends to help preserve a "dignified" transition—friends like former secretary of state Henry Kissinger, former Citigroup chairman Sandy Weill, and Blackstone Group head Pete Peterson.

Then came the Easter weekend documents caper.

It happened in Bermuda, where AIG had sensitive facilities. On Good Friday, a lawyer for Greenberg carted boxes of documents out of an AIG office and into a van. The next day, lawyers working for the firm discovered that certain documents were missing. More surprising, they discovered an AIG employee had destroyed some computer records and tape recordings of business meetings. There was a confrontation between Greenberg's lawyers and the company's lawyers, and word quickly reached Eliot Spitzer, who was skiing in Colorado.

Spitzer called Beattie, and finally issued his ultimatum. "As long as Hank is still the chairman, AIG is still accountable," he said. "You have serious criminal exposure." Spitzer then dropped the bomb. He said he would indict the company on Monday if action wasn't taken.

The board scheduled another meeting in Beattie's office on Monday, with most members attending by phone, and all knowing the inevitable outcome.

Just minutes before the meeting began, Greenberg had his attorney, David Boies, fax in his letter of resignation as chairman of AIG. The man who had built AIG from scratch had now severed all ties.

9 ||||||||||||||||||||||||||||||||

Harry Stonecipher met with his directors the morning after they learned of his interoffice romance, and quickly acknowledged his guilt.

"Am I having an affair? Yes," he said. "I've been married for 50 years—the last 15 in name only. I have achieved a lot of business success. I've made a lot of money. I'm entitled to some happiness.

"Do I think I did anything wrong?" he continued. "No. But if you think I embarrassed the company, that's your decision to make."

The response was classic Stonecipher—straight, no-nonsense—but it was also stunning to members of the board. They all knew his wife Joan, who accompanied him to numerous board meetings and other events. One board member asked how long the relationship had been going on. Stonecipher replied that it had started at the annual get-together of about 250 top Boeing managers at Palm Springs. He adamantly denied, however, that he had improperly helped the career of the executive involved, or used company resources to carry out the affair.

In some ways, it was the e-mails that the board members found most surprising. They raised serious questions about Stonecipher's judgment. It was one thing to carry on a discreet relationship out of the eyeshot of colleagues. But it was quite another to be sending such graphic, even sophomoric, e-mails on his BlackBerry, presumably during company meetings.

Moreover, Stonecipher had every reason to know that such

e-mails were far from private. His predecessor, Phil Condit, had been
fired partly as a result of e-mails that were recovered by investigators
from his computer's hard drive. And Senator John McCain had had
a field day with e-mails the investigation had turned up, indicating
inappropriate contacts with the government. If there was one lesson
the top folks at Boeing should have learned over the previous two
years it was this: Unlike love, e-mails are forever. Don't write anything in them you wouldn't want read on the Jumbotron at Times
Square.

Particularly troubling to board members was that the issue of
corporate ethics was at the very center of Stonecipher's leadership.
If all was true, how could he continue to lead the change at Boeing?
How would the company's critics in Congress—like Senator John
McCain—react when they found out about it? Savvier members of
the board realized quickly that they *would* find out about it. It was
not clear who had sent the extraordinary letter to Lewis Platt accus-
ing Stonecipher, but the board had every reason to assume that
whoever sent it was willing to send it to the press if the board didn't
respond.

Board members asked to meet with Bonnie Soodik, because she
ran the ethics program and also had received a copy of the letter.
She had been close to Stonecipher, having worked for him previously at McDonnell Douglas, and when she met with the board, she
was clearly distraught.

At some point in the discussion, a board member asked her,
"How can you administer an ethics program for 160,000 employees
if it's perceived that your CEO is above the rules?"

Soodik started to shake. She looked like she was about to cry.
Finally, she answered:

"I can't."

In the end, it was those two words that sealed Harry Stonecipher's fate. Some board members were reluctant to move, and

wanted to proceed slowly and deliberately. Dozens of CEOs, they figured, had had affairs with their underlings. Moreover, Stonecipher was clearly good for the company. Another scandal now might be more than Boeing could take.

Ken Duberstein, who had weathered numerous political scandals, understood the mechanics of scandal control. There was only one course of action that made sense, he said. Deal with the problem quickly and decisively, before it becomes public—which, inevitably, it will.

The previous year, Duberstein had lived through the problems at Fannie Mae, the government-chartered mortgage finance company that had come under attack for its accounting practices. He had been part of a group that had fired former CEO Franklin Raines. He understood better than most that CEOs were becoming increasingly like politicians, dependent on the goodwill of the public to flourish. And he understood that sitting on corporate boards was no longer just an honor; it had become a heavy responsibility. If the board allowed Stonecipher to stay and his affair became public, directors would come under attack. How could they know about this, and do nothing.

Duberstein laid out the reasons why Harry had to go, and to go quickly. By the time the board left the meeting, the conclusion seemed inevitable.

Over the course of the next few days, a law firm hired by Platt investigated the affair. On Stonecipher's computer hard drive, lawyers found more explicit e-mails. None of them indicated the CEO had used corporate resources to carry out the affair. He had gone to Washington on a couple of occasions—once to attend the annual Alfalfa dinner with Duberstein—and had met up with Debra Peabody while there, but he hadn't used corporate jets solely for the purpose of meeting her. (The board later learned, on the other hand, that Peabody did arrange several business meetings on

Fridays in Chicago, so she could spend the weekend with Stone-cipher.)

Knowing that managing public and congressional relations would prove key to escaping this latest scandal, Platt brought two people into his confidence—Todd Hullin, head of public relations, and Rudy DeLeone, head of the Washington office. By week's end, there was agreement. Stonecipher would go. James Bell, the current chief financial officer, would take the job temporarily while directors searched for a replacement. Platt would get more deeply involved in helping to manage the company in the meantime.

Platt decided that key legislators and people in the administration should be contacted before the news became public. The calls went out Sunday night. Ken Duberstein called Senator John McCain, who had been the company's chief critic.

McCain was surprised. "Harry was in my office last Thursday," he responded. "Now I know why he was smiling."

Monday morning, the press release went out: "The Board actions were taken following an investigation by internal and external legal counsel of the facts and circumstances surrounding a personal relationship between Stonecipher and a female executive of the company who did not report directly to him."

"The Board concluded that the facts reflected poorly on Harry's judgment and would impair his ability to lead the company," Platt was quoted as saying.

In just nine short days, Harry Stonecipher, the man hired to salvage Boeing's reputation, was gone.

10 ||||||||||||||||||||||||||

Carly Fiorina. Hank Greenberg. Harry Stonecipher.

Their stories are all different in the details. But it is no accident that they all lost their jobs, running three of America's most powerful corporations, within the same few weeks at the beginning of 2005. All three were acting according to the rules they had learned in the final decades of the 20th century—the heyday of corporate power. In the first five years of the 21st century, those rules changed, catching Fiorina, Greenberg and Stonecipher by surprise.

And they weren't alone.

Franklin Raines, an African American who rose from childhood poverty to become a Rhodes Scholar, hold a top post in the Clinton administration, and finally to be the chairman and chief executive at mortgage giant Fannie Mae, had been ousted from his job just four days before Christmas in 2004.

Like Hank Greenberg's AIG, Fannie Mae was known as a company that made its own rules. Located in Washington, D.C., and originally chartered by Congress, it boasted one of the most powerful lobbying machines that city had ever seen. It rewarded its friends and won over its enemies by giving them grants from its foundation or, often, cushy jobs at its sprawling offices. On Wall Street, it was praised not only for managing financial risk, but for managing "political risk"—a polite way of saying that it almost always got its way. Former treasury secretary Lawrence Summers once said that whenever there was a whiff of a thought at Treasury to rein in the company's favored status, Fannie would mount "a man-to-man defense—Frank would call me, his deputy would call my deputy, his number three would call my number three, his janitor would call the Treasury janitor."

In return for all this, Raines was paid lavishly, collecting more than $20 million in 2002 and 2003.

One sign of Fannie Mae's immense clout was the fact that it had successfully lobbied Congress to keep its regulator housed at the Department of Housing and Urban Development—a weak agency whose job was to promote housing, not regulate financial institutions—rather than at the stronger Treasury Department. But in the changed climate of the post-Enron period, an obscure head of the HUD office, Armando Falcon Jr., decided to take on the mortgage giant and challenge its accounting.

In a report that landed with a heavy thud in September of 2004, he accused the company of "pervasive" errors in accounting for the firm's large portfolio of financial derivatives. He pointed directly at top managers, saying they prized smoothly rising earnings and allowed weak internal controls. Falcon also showed how in some years, the accounting misstatements helped ensure that Raines and company received multimillion-dollar bonuses.

The criticism involved a fairly arcane corner of the accounting rules, where interpretations could differ. Raines denounced the regulator and insisted that "the company is in fine shape." He said he was confident the Securities and Exchange Commission would find Fannie had done nothing wrong, and promised to take responsibility if the SEC found otherwise.

But on December 15, the chief accountant of the SEC sided with Falcon. Fannie had violated the accounting rules and would have to restate its earnings for the past four years, recognizing an estimated $9 billion of losses on derivatives.

Before the week was out, the board met and decided Raines had to go as well.

Three months earlier, the most powerful executive in Holly-wood—Michael Eisner—announced he would leave his post as chief executive of the Walt Disney Company, finally succumbing in an extraordinary battle against his leadership.

Eisner's demise was much less abrupt than that of Raines, Fiorina, Greenberg, and Stonecipher. Indeed, it resulted from a decade of poor performance and controversial leadership. The performance problem was encapsulated in a sagging stock price, lackluster earnings, and a lack of big hits—the company of Mickey Mouse hadn't had a blockbuster animated film since *The Lion King* in 1994. The leadership problem was best symbolized by his 1997 decision to fire former superagent Michael Ovitz, who after only 14 months on the job as president walked away with hundreds of millions of dollars of shareholders' money.

Still, Eisner managed to hold on. It was not until Roy Disney, the son of the company's founder, launched a shareholder war against Eisner reminiscent of Walter Hewlett's battle against Carly Fiorina, that Eisner's edifice began to crack. As the March 2004 shareholder meeting approached, the nation's largest public pension fund—the California Public Employees' Retirement System, or CalPERS—announced it had "lost complete confidence in Eisner's strategic vision and leadership" and would withhold voting for his reelection to the board. Others followed suit, including the California State Teachers' Retirement System and the New York State Common Retirement Fund. The firms that advise institutional shareholders—Institutional Shareholder Services in Rockville, Maryland, and Glass, Lewis and Company in San Francisco—joined the "vote no" coalition.

The result was an unprecedented 43 percent vote withheld from Eisner at the annual meeting—not enough to remove him, but enough to signal that something had to change. Eisner gave up the chairman's post to former senator George Mitchell. Still, it was clear that wasn't enough to satisfy his critics, so in early September, he agreed to step down.

Even as Fiorina and Greenberg and Stonecipher were entering their forced retirement, Morgan Stanley chief Philip Purcell was desperately trying to prevent his.

Purcell had long been a controversial figure on Wall Street. He had been the head of Dean Witter, Discover and Company when it merged with Morgan Stanley back in 1997, and had nudged out veteran John Mack in 2001 to hold on to the top job. But among the firm's investment bankers, he had never found much support. He was aloof, surrounded himself with loyalists, purged potential challengers, and never moved from Chicago, commuting back from New York on most weekends. In late 2004, when he began to get a whiff of dissent, he waived the board's retirement rules to bring back 71-year-old Edward Brennan, the former CEO of Sears Roebuck and a dependable loyalist.

For Purcell, things started to unravel in early 2005, when a former Morgan Stanley executive turned hedge fund manager, Scott Sipprelle, launched a public broadside against the company. Sipprelle urged the firm to dump a number of its businesses, noting the stock had fallen 4 percent in 2004 while other investment banks soared. Sipprelle was particularly critical of Purcell, who earned $22 million in compensation in 2004.

Then in late March, eight former investment bankers at Morgan Stanley—all major shareholders—launched an extraordinary attack of their own to oust Purcell. The unlikely revolutionaries were led by Parker Gilbert, who at 71 was typical of the old-school, white-shoe ways of a former age of Wall Street, and by Robert Scott, age 59. Appearing on television, Scott insisted, "We are not going to go away," and Gilbert said, "Time is of the essence."

The Morgan Stanley board, like Purcell himself, was slow to recognize the new dynamic in corporate America. Directors dismissed

Gilbert, Scott and company as a bunch of grumpy old men, who still resented the merger of eight years earlier. "It struck us that the complaints against Phil were more personal than based on performance," said Michael Miles, a former CEO of Philip Morris Companies and a Morgan Stanley director.

In the weeks that followed, however, the attacks against Purcell multiplied. The Council of Institutional Investors, which represents large pension funds, called for talks with Purcell over the situation. High-level Morgan Stanley employees left the firm to take jobs elsewhere. Perhaps most important, the hedge funds, sensing blood, began to move in. These fast-moving pools of money would buy up shares in a company like Morgan Stanley when they sensed change was afoot, in hopes of profiting from a spike in the stock.

In early June, three of Morgan Stanley's directors traveled to Boston and heard a stern critique from the leaders of one of those hedge funds, Highfields Capital Management LP. Unless Purcell resigned, they were told, he risked a Disney-style shareholder revolt at the company's annual meeting in 2006.

On June 13, Purcell announced he would resign. He left the firm on June 30.

No industry felt the winds of change more violently than the pharmaceutical business. The big drug companies had once been a key component of any savvy investor's portfolio. They were money-making machines, selling drugs that, in some cases, people needed to survive, or at least thrive, and doing it under the protection of patents, which reduced competition.

By 2005, however, the pipeline of blockbuster drugs was running dry. Moreover, consumers were growing increasingly angry about the high cost of those drugs. The rise of the Internet made it increasingly apparent to Americans that the same drugs they paid a premium for in the United States could be purchased in countries that controlled drug prices—Canada, for instance—at a fraction of the cost. On top of that, there were signs that some of the block-buster drugs had nasty side effects, and an army of trial lawyers was ready to pounce on any that could conceivably be blamed for caus-ing deaths.

That combination of financial and regulatory pressures became fatal for the CEOs of drug companies in 2005 and 2006.

Merck CEO Raymond Gilmartin became the first to fall. Al-though he was widely recognized as the most open and in some ways most progressive of the big Pharma leaders, his company got caught in a firestorm over its painkiller, Vioxx, which was linked to heart problems and prompted a tidal wave of litigation. Gilmartin, who became chairman and CEO in 1994, had been expected to stay on the job until March of 2006. The troubles with Vioxx, and the fact that the company had failed to develop a healthy pipeline of new drugs, caused many shareholders to turn against him.

A search panel made up of three independent members of the board chose a Merck insider, Richard Clark, to replace him as chief executive. Gilmartin didn't participate in the search, or in the board conference call at which Clark was elected. He wasn't asked to stay on as chairman, either. Instead the company said it would go with-out a chairman for a year or two, while a special three-person board executive committee would advise Clark.

Pfizer CEO Hank McKinnell was next to fall. He had watched the demise of his rival, Gilmartin, and thought that he had successfully avoided that fate. In early 2006, his board expressed full confidence in his leadership. But like Merck, Pfizer faced the problem of expir-ing patents on its blockbuster drugs and an uninspiring pipeline of products to replace them. Moreover, McKinnell became the tar-get of a fierce campaign over his compensation. A Dallas investor by the name of Frederick "Shad" Rowe joined with investor advo-cate T. Boone Pickens to form a new group called the Investors for Director Accountability Project. The group made McKinnell their first target.

The problem, the group pointed out, using figures calculated by the Corporate Library, was that Pfizer shareholders had seen their stock drop by 40 percent over a five-year period. In that same period, McKinnell had earned some $79 million in pay and bonuses, and a pension of $6 million a year for life. When I wrote about this in April, director Stanley Ikenberry valiantly tried to defend those numbers to me by arguing that big Pharma companies were going through a tough transition, and McKinnell was doing a good job leading that transition.

Three months later, however, McKinnell was gone—a year ahead of his planned retirement. Unlike Gilmartin, he was permitted to stay on the board until February of 2007.

Just a few months after McKinnell's departure, another CEO—Peter Dolan of Bristol-Myers Squibb—got the axe. His shareholders, like those of Pfizer and Merck, had suffered from years of no stock appreciation. On the verge of losing patent protection for its blockbuster heart drug, Plavix, the company attempted to negotiate a deal with a Canadian firm to keep a low-priced generic off the market. The deal backfired, clearing the way for the generic and attracting a Justice Department antitrust investigation in the process.

The heat on Dolan ratcheted up quickly. Business blogs were filled with obscenity-laced postings denouncing his tenure. Some large shareholders demanded his head. CNBC's sputtering money maven Jim Cramer called the executive the "single worst CEO" in his shareholder-value-destroying Hall of Shame. Finally, a court-appointed monitor, placed at Bristol-Myers Squibb following an earlier scandal, told the directors what they had already concluded on their own—Dolan had to go.

CEO critics still liked to talk about the evils of "entrenched" corporate management. But it was clear to anyone paying attention that CEOs were no longer entrenched. According to research by Burson-Marsteller, CEO turnover was up 126 percent in 2005 over 2000. Booz Allen Hamilton said 35 percent of North American CEOs who left in 2005 were forced out of their jobs, up from just 12 percent a decade earlier.

To those who occupied top CEO positions, it was abundantly clear that their power and prestige had suffered a steep decline. Being CEO still had its advantages—multimillion-dollar paychecks were one of them—but the job was a lot less secure and a lot more precarious than it had ever been in the past.

CHAPTER TWO

THE BATTLE FOR THE CORPORATION

1

Private property—*ownership*—is at the core of the capitalist system.

But who owns public corporations?

We talk about shareholders as owners. But the truth is, they have few of the rights or the obligations that are normally associated with the ownership of private property. They are, on the one hand, shielded from the liability that normally goes with property ownership. And on the other, they lack most of the basic privileges of ownership, such as, for instance, the right of entry. Try getting into the headquarters of any major corporation by waiving a stock certificate and saying, "Hey, I own this place."

So what, exactly, is the relationship between the share "owner" and the company?

Until the stock market collapse of 1929, the answer was simple. If a shareholder didn't like what was going on in the corporation, he or she had one recourse: sell the stock. Ownership was a vague promise of future dividends. If you believed in that promise, you would hang on to the stock. If you lost faith, you dumped it.

But the collapse of the stock market in 1929 forced a rethinking of that relationship. Over the preceding decades, ownership of stock had become a widespread phenomenon. Estimates of the number of Americans who owned some stock at the time of the Great Crash range from three million to seven million. Millions more were affected by the failure of banks and insurance companies that had invested their funds in Wall Street. The crash left all those shareholders feeling badly burned.

In 1932, on the heels of the Great Crash, a lawyer—Adolf Berle—and an academic—Gardiner Means—analyzed the conundrum of share ownership in a landmark work that became the most influential book ever to be written about the corporation: *The Modern Corporation and Private Property*. As Berle and Means saw it, modern society had evolved from private ownership of the means of production, to corporate ownership—a "corporate system." Corporations had become, in Thorstein Veblen's phrase, the "master instruments of civilization." Shareholders had largely surrendered control over their own wealth to the corporation, and in the process "had broken the old property relationships" and "raised the problem of defining these relationships anew."

Berle and Means distinguished between the "private corporation," owned by a relatively small group of shareholders who exercised tight control, and the "quasi public" corporation, where shareholding was widely dispersed. Increasingly, they noted, the quasi-public corporation was becoming the norm. As an example, they cited the American Telephone and Telegraph Company, "perhaps the most advanced development of the corporate system. With assets of almost five billions dollars, with 454,000 employes, and stockholders to the number of 567,694, this company may indeed be called an economic empire—an empire bounded by no geographical limits, but held together by centralized control."

The fundamental problem of the new system, Berle and Means argued, is that "the separation of ownership from control produces a condition where the interests of owner and of ultimate manager may, and often do, diverge, and where many of the checks which formerly operated to limit the use of power disappear."

This was the central problem of corporations—that the interests of owners and managers were not the same. The result was an enormous concentration of power in the hands of managers—"comparable to the concentration of religious power in the mediaeval church or of political power in the national state." That absolute power may be "useful in building the organization." But over time, they argued, it would eventually give way to abuse by managers, who would inevitably divert the corporation's resources to their own uses.

Berle and Means suggest two directions in which the corporate system might evolve. One was to increase the rights of the shareholders, so that they would have the power to ensure the company is run for the owners' benefit, rather than the managers'. The other was to recognize the corporation as a quasi-public institution, and have society demand the corporation not just serve the owners or the managers, but all of society—a kind of corporate socialism.

The publication of Berle and Means's book can be seen as the start of the great battle for control of the corporation. In the decades that followed, activist shareholders struggled, often in futility, to increase their control over the corporation, while various others tried, with decidedly mixed results, to force companies to respond to the demands of "society." At the core of these battles, always, was the struggle between the interests of owners and managers.

Shortly after the publication of Berle and Means's book, Congress undertook its first major effort to reform the corporate world. The Securities Act of 1933 and the Securities Exchange Act of 1934 were designed to make the operations of giant corporations more transparent to their owners. Congress provided for the registration of corporate securities and set rules for providing information to shareholders. It also set up a basic framework to protect shareholders from outright fraud. In doing so, the law also took a step toward acknowledging society's interest in providing a check to unrestrained corporate power. And it endorsed the notion of shareholder suffrage as a right that attached to any stock bought on a public exchange.

Still, for all the attention they attracted, those New Deal laws did relatively little to resolve the basic tension between owners and managers. "Shareholder resolutions," for instance—which later became a major means by which owners might express their disagreements with management—are nowhere mentioned in the law. Shareholder power was more of an ideal than a reality.

2 ||||||||||||||||||||||||||||||||

It took a crusader, Lewis Gilbert, to turn the vague language of the new laws into a tool for action. Gilbert had inherited enough money to enable him to pursue his crusade, but not enough to withstand another 1929-style assault. So after the crash, he began to campaign on behalf of shareholders.

As he recalled later: "In the early days of the New Deal, I realized the time was right to get something for us, the shareholders, and not just for the socialists and all those other people. We needed a forum of our own."

It was a frustrating crusade. At first, his demands were fairly simple—for instance, he pushed to have the annual shareholders meetings held at locations more readily accessible to shareholders. But still, he was almost always rebuffed. At a 1933 stockholders meeting, he tried to raise a question, only to be ignored by the chair who adjourned the meeting by inviting stockholders to a buffet. As one of the company's "owners," Gilbert was incensed. "I had been publicly humiliated by my own employees," he said. "I was treated like a tramp who could be put off with a handout."

Still, he continued his quixotic campaign. A breakthrough came in 1939, when he complained to the new SEC that Bethlehem Steel had not disclosed to shareholders in its proxy statement Gilbert's intention to present two resolutions at the company's annual meeting—one seeking to move the next year's meeting to New York, and the other giving shareholders the right to approve corporate auditors. The SEC, still trying to find its purpose, took the opportunity to step in, and forced Bethlehem Steel to reschedule its meeting and reissue proxies with proper notification of Gilbert's proposals. That was the birth of the principal tool of shareholder activists—the proxy resolution.

CEOs were appalled—they saw the SEC's intrusion as endorsing a form of corporate bolshevism. At a minimum, they thought, the measure opened the door to troublemakers and cranks. And indeed, on that point, they were half right. Gilbert soon was joined by his younger brother John in his continuing crusade, and they became celebrities, of sorts, in the financial world. He once got into a shouting match with Charles Schwab after suggesting the steel magnate should go without pay after Bethlehem had a bad year. On another occasion, the chairman of Chemical Bank threatened to punch him in the nose for impertinence.

Gilbert's crusade attracted imitators—like Wilma Soss, founder of the Federation of Women Shareholders. She shared many of Gilbert's goals, but also had a social cause: getting women appointed to boards of directors. In 1948, she began protesting the fact that U.S. Steel held its annual meetings in Hoboken, New Jersey. Traveling to Hoboken constitutes a "mental hazard," particularly for women, she complained. "It may be an unusual thought to you gentlemen, but U.S. Steel is a woman's company," she said. "You have over 5 percent more women than men stockholders." When the company rebuffed her request, she dressed in a Gay Nineties costume and arrived at the annual meeting "dressed to match management thinking." On another occasion, she arrived at the New York Central meeting in Chicago dressed entirely in black. She told the executives there that she did so "to mourn attempts to kill instead of promote passenger service."

Gilbert and Soss became perennial gadflies at corporate annual meetings, sometimes getting ejected jointly by irritated board chairmen. In the late 1950s, they were joined by Evelyn Y. Davis, who took their antics to new heights. She once accused an executive of "Nazi" tactics, and admonished Chrysler CEO Lee Iacocca to watch his diet. She published an idiosyncratic newsletter, "Highlights and Lowlights," and got CEOs, hoping to avoid her attacks, to pay for subscriptions.

While Soss had a social agenda—the advancement of women— she, like Gilbert and Davis, was principally an advocate of shareholders' economic rights. But in the 1970s, the momentum shifted to crusaders who were only incidentally shareholders. Rather, they saw corporate power as a means to achieve social goals.

James Peck was the forerunner of these social advocates. In 1948, he launched a campaign against Greyhound for its practice of segregated seating on buses. He bought a share of stock in Greyhound in order to raise the issue at the 1948 annual meeting in Wilmington, Delaware, and reintroduced the issue as a shareholder resolution each year for the next three years. Meanwhile, organized labor was also getting into the act. The AITU (precursor to the Communications Workers of America) bought shares of stock of AT&T to protest the company's move to cut pension benefits.

The number of shareholder resolutions grew fairly slowly in the 1950s and 1960s, from about 100 in the mid-'50s to about 200 by the end of the 1960s. Then came 1970. As anti–Vietnam War sentiment swelled, and social activism rose, corporations became a target too tempting to miss.

On April 28 of that year, 300 screaming young demonstrators forced adjournment of the Honeywell annual meeting in Minneapolis only 14 minutes after it was called to order. The protesters objected to the company's production of cluster bombs.

The same day in Pittsburgh, 30–40 protesters gained admission to the Gulf Oil Corporation annual meeting with stock proxies, and shouted intermittently during the two-hour meeting. Their demand: that the company should terminate all defense contracts and stop doing business in colonial Angola.

The day before in Chicago, 160 new stockholders attended the annual meeting of Commonwealth Edison Company to protest the company's continuing contribution to air pollution, and a crowd of demonstrators attempted to disrupt the annual meeting of the Boeing Company in Seattle.

The big event was the 1970 annual meeting of the General Motors Corporation, held on May 22 in Detroit. Three months earlier, consumer crusader Ralph Nader announced plans for a "Campaign GM." His group was backed by an association of young lawyers in Washington called the Project on Corporate Responsibility. It managed to get the SEC to agree that two of its nine original proposals had to be placed on the company's proxy. The two measures called on GM to add three new "public" members to its board, and to create a "committee on corporate responsibility."

Among those to object to Nader's tactics were Lewis Gilbert and Wilma Soss. In an interview with the *Chicago Tribune,* they questioned Nader's commitment to the capitalist system, asking whether he was a "raider" or a "guerilla." Gilbert said political questions, like support for the Vietnam War, had no place at annual meetings. Evelyn Y. Davis had an even stronger reaction. "Nader should stick to his own thing," she sniffed. "Let me handle the stockholders' meeting. Let him handle things in Washington."

The GM meeting was packed with nearly 3,000 people, many of

them students wearing blue jeans, who had arrived early and in some cases brought a picnic lunch. Many either owned only a few GM shares, or had used others' proxies to get into the meeting. Not to be upstaged, Davis stripped down to a bathing suit, and marched around the room waving an American flag. The protesters fired questions at a visibly nervous James M. Roche, chairman and chief executive of GM.

Barbara Williams, a black law student from the University of California at Los Angeles, asked him why GM hadn't any black directors. "Because none have been elected," Roche replied. That wasn't adequate, she responded. "Black people buy your products, we breathe the air you pollute. Why are there no blacks on your board?"

The impact of the reformers was diluted by Gilbert and Davis, who managed to get hold of one of the six microphones scattered around the hall with surprising regularity. In a strange instance of role reversal, they alternately supported management, stressed the traditional goals of shareholders for higher profits and dividends, and openly attacked the goals of the reformers as "the beginnings of the end of the capitalist system."

In the end, more than 97 percent of the votes cast opposed the Nader group's two shareholder resolutions. The great GM showdown showed that the situation had changed little since Berle and Means wrote their book nearly four decades earlier. The activists had managed to turn the annual corporate meeting into an entertaining circus. But even they were split on whether the company needed to be more responsive to the demands of shareholders or more attentive to the needs of society. Meanwhile, managers were still very much in control.

3 ||||||||||||||||||||||||||||||

As I've argued throughout this book, corporations are political institutions. They are creations of the state, and ultimately rely on the support of the public to survive and thrive. They lost that support after the stock market crash of 1929 and during the depression of the 1930s, and they lost it again during the social upheaval of the 1970s.

As a result, companies felt compelled to gradually pay more attention to the activists. In part, this was an effort to head off the embarrassment that came from large protest votes—like that which faced the Chrysler Company, when 20 percent of votes cast supported a shareholder resolution to tighten up executive compensation.

In 1977, for instance, AT&T, which had always stoutly opposed all stockholder resolutions, finally agreed to support a measure calling for secret balloting at annual meetings. A similar measure had failed five times in the past, and had won only 3.4 percent of the vote in the previous year. But AT&T felt the annual fights were a distraction, and decided to give in.

That same year, the American Jewish Congress withdrew shareholder proposals after negotiating agreements with several large companies—including Gulf Oil, Bethlehem Steel, Goodyear Tire and Rubber, Standard Oil of California, and Tenneco—which said they would provide information about their response to the Arab boycott of Israel. Exxon management supported a resolution, submitted by a group of churches, calling for disclosure of its strip-mining activities.

And Mobil Oil Corporation announced that it would take two actions suggested by stockholders—requiring all outside directors to sign a conflict-of-interest statement and redesigning its proxy card so shareholders could vote for some but not necessarily all of the nominees for board seats.

In part, the activists' successes were spurred by the involvement of more mainstream organizations, like the Interfaith Center on Corporate Responsibility, a group formed at the beginning of the 1970s to help Roman Catholic groups leverage their stock holdings. The center aimed to stop a wide variety of corporate activities— including television violence, sales of military equipment, nuclear power expansion, the sale of baby formula in other countries, and so on. But the social activists achieved their greatest success in the campaign against support for the apartheid regime of South Africa.

Since the days of James Peck, race had always been a powerful issue for those wishing to turn corporate power to the purpose of addressing social goals. In 1966, Saul Alinsky helped a community group in Rochester, New York, convince the owners of 39,000 Kodak shares to sign over their proxies, so they could be used to vote against current management for failing to hire minorities. In the end, the company agreed to implement a minority hiring program accepted by the dissidents.

The campaign to get companies to cut off South Africa started off slowly. In 1978, the Reverend Howard Schomer appeared at the annual meeting of the First National Boston Corporation to oppose bank loans to South Africa until the countries "racist laws and regulation have been revoked and meaningful steps have been taken in the direction of majority rule." The bank successfully opposed the measure. Similarly, Mobil Oil Corporation fought off a measure backed by church groups to cut oil shipments to South Africa. And Motorola Inc. opposed a resolution submitted by Haverford College to stop supplying radios and other electronic equipment to the South African police. The prevailing view in the corporate community was that expressed by D. J. Kirchhoff, president and chief executive of Castle & Cooke Inc., who told a group of financial writers in 1979 that he opposed shareholder groups who "use corporate annual meetings as a primary battleground" for "divisive and abrasive" political and social issues.

"More business leaders are beginning to speak up on this," Kirchhoff said. "They aren't going to let these charges go unanswered." While most business leaders were unwilling to speak as openly as Kirchhoff, they generally shared the view expressed by the *Wall Street Journal* editorial page:

> *Most U.S. businesses in South Africa are expounding the sensible view—we provide goods and services to our customers and profits to our investors; we obey the local laws and try not to do anything beastly, and politics is the politicians' business.*

That didn't stop the shareholder activists. They kept offering shareholder resolutions, and kept getting ever larger—if still not majority—votes on their resolutions. Churches and universities joined forces to use the power of their investments to put pressure on companies. In 1986, for instance, the board of trustees of Stanford University, responding to student and faculty pressure, voted to divest from two companies with interests in South Africa—the first time the university had ever divested because of a social issue. Other universities did the same.

Pension funds also jumped in. The New York City and New York State public employees funds began supporting resolutions to sell shares of companies operating in South Africa. The Teachers' Insurance and Annuity Association/College Retirement

Equities Fund—the giant $30 billion fund for college and university professors—also took a prominent role.

By the mid-1980s, hundreds of companies responded to the pressure, by adopting the so-called "Sullivan Principles"—named after activist minister and General Motors director Leon Sullivan—requiring signatories to treat their black and white employees equally, no matter where they did business. By 1985, all but two of the top 50 of Fortune 500 companies doing business in South Africa had signed on.

From there, the campaigns continued to ratchet up the pressure, calling on companies to divest entirely. Big cities, like New York, San Francisco and Los Angeles, jumped into the act with divestment legislation, and a number of states, including California and Massachusetts, followed suit. Corporations responded, and by 1989, South Africa responded as well. Apartheid was brought to an end. Corporate activism alone wasn't the reason for the South African government's retreat, but it certainly played an important role. In the process, the activists had found a potent tool for pursuing other causes.

Despite their successes, the social activists of the 1970s were just an annoyance to the managers of big corporations, not a real threat to their power. A much more serious threat came in the early 1980s, with the rise of corporate raiders, like Carl Icahn and T. Boone Pickens.

These raiders had planted their roots back in 1974, when Morgan Stanley, a prestigious investment bank, advised two clients to launch hostile takeover bids. Inco, the nickel company, mounted a bid to take over a Philadelphia-based maker of batteries, ESB, and later, Philips NV went after Magnavox. Up to that point, hostile takeovers had been rare. Mergers occurred only when the managers of both companies agreed. But Morgan Stanley's attacks changed that.

The rise of the raiders created an unaccustomed threat for corporate managers, and it underscored the divergent interests of managers and shareholders. The raiders paid a premium for the stock, offering shareholders a chance to make money. But the managers were more interested in retaining control, and thus usually rebuffed the raiders. In many cases, they sought out "white knights" to merge with, and prevent the takeover.

In 1981, for instance, Seagram made a billion-dollar hostile bid for St. Joseph Minerals. To escape, St. Joseph arranged a merger with Fluor for $2.7 billion. Later that year, Seagram went after Conoco, sparking a vicious battle that eventually delivered the oil company to white knight DuPont for a record $8 billion.

What really angered shareholders, however, were the tactics increasingly adopted by companies to make the raiders go away. In 1980, Gulf & Western, a devourer of other companies, bought a 7.4 percent stake in Oxford Industries and a 10.4 percent stake in Robertshaw Controls Company saying they were for "investment" purposes. Two months later, Oxford and Robertshaw bought back their shares for $2.1 million more than Gulf & Western paid for them. The two companies, in effect, used the money of the vast majority of their shareholders to buy off the one that was causing trouble. Bruce Wasserstein, an investment banker whose specialty was mergers, compared the payments to "ransom." Later, it came to be known as "greenmail."

The two leading raiders of the 1980s, Pickens and Icahn, both built fortunes out of greenmail. In 1979, for instance, a group headed by Icahn announced it had acquired slightly less than 10 percent of the stock of Saxon Industries. At a meeting with company management, Icahn bluntly told company president Stanley Lurie that Saxon could either buy him out or face a proxy fight. Soon afterward, Saxon agreed to buy back 766,700 shares from Icahn's group at $10.50 a share—well above the group's cost of $7.20.

Icahn had grown up in a lower-middle-class section of Queens, New York. His mother was a schoolteacher, his father a lawyer, teacher and a cantor. He became the first student from his high school to attend Princeton University, where he joined one of the school's eating clubs. But in his new game, he was out to break up the comfortable club of American corporate management, for his own benefit.

In 1982, Icahn threatened to take over Hammermill Paper. To retain its independence, the company agreed to buy back Icahn's shares at a steep premium over market price—a premium not available to other shareholders. Over the next two years, he was able to get similar greenmail payments from Marshall Field's, Dan River and American Can.

For Icahn, this "greenmail" was an easy way to build a fortune. For other shareholders, it was an outrageous rip-off—and showed just how weak their "ownership" of the corporation really was. The corporate managers denied shareholders the potential premium that could come from a takeover, and then used their money to make the raider go away.

The raider movement got its biggest boost in 1983. At Drexel Burnham Lambert's spring conference, Michael Milken made a radical proposal. He had been pioneering the use of high-yield "junk" bonds for companies that lacked high-quality credit. Why not use those junk bonds, he argued, to finance hostile takeovers? With the leverage those bonds offered, relatively small players could take on giant companies. Indeed, raiders could borrow 100 percent of the money needed to win the takeover battle.

Recognizing the opportunity, Boone Pickens took Milken up on his offer and launched fights for control of Gulf Oil and Phillips Petroleum Company. After buying off Pickens at a premium, Phillips then faced another buyout proposal from Icahn. "Corporate raiders, like Boone Pickens and Carl Icahn, have bent the plowshares of free enterprise into the swords of economic chaos," complained C. M. Kittrell, an executive vice president of Phillips.

The takeover frenzy continued to accelerate in the mid-1980s, with Ron Perelman buying up companies with junk debt, then stripping them of assets to pay off the debt. To escape raiders, companies increasingly arranged mergers of their own. In 1985 alone, Icahn took over TWA, Philip Morris took over General Foods, and Procter & Gamble took over Richardson-Vicks. And all three TV networks changed hands as a result of deals or raid attempts. Greenmail payments also became more frequent and larger. In 1984, Walt Disney Productions paid financier Saul Steinberg a $60 million premium to go away. Felix Rohatyn, who had helped Harold Geneen build his empire in the 1960s, said the takeover trend of the 1980s made those years "look like Little Lord Fauntleroy."

The raiders, almost all men, became consumed in the frantic work that made them fortunes. Many came to see the corporate battles in personal terms. "Weekends, vacations, personal commitments and families all take a back seat when a hostile battle is raging," wrote Leslie Wayne in the *New York Times*. "They have even developed their own language, laced with the images of aggression and sexual conquest: raids, battles, white knights, wooing, shark repellent, bear hugs." Hostile raids were compared to rape. White knight mergers were the result of a company deciding "who do I want to get into bed with." As one female executive at Conoco put it: "You get the feeling that this is the ultimate macho game."

The takeover frenzy sparked a lively debate over corporate control. Attorney Martin Lipton, who was the favorite consigliere of managers under attack, argued that the takeover craze forced companies to take measures that improved their market price "by emphasizing short-run profits at the expense of long-term planning." He helped countless companies adopt "poison pills" that made it increasingly costly for a company to be taken over.

But raiders like Pickens dismissed that argument as an excuse. "It is questionable how much more long-term planning shareholders can stand," he wrote "What many managements seem to be demanding is more time to keep making the same mistakes." Richard Darman, serving as Ronald Reagan's deputy secretary of the treasury, praised Icahn and Pickens as a "new kind of populist folk hero," and noted that "large-scale corporate America" had a "tendency to be like the government bureaucracy that corporate executives love to malign: bloated, risk-averse, inefficient and unimaginative." The raiders were changing that.

While the raiders threatened corporate power from the outside, a growing group of managers discovered the same tactics could be used to enrich those on the inside. If Carl Icahn or Boone Pickens could buy their company with junk debt and reap the profits, why shouldn't they do the same thing themselves? "Management buyouts" became increasingly common. In these deals, a company's managers would team up with a buyout firm, issue junk bonds, and use the proceeds to buy back all their company's shares. This would free them entirely from the pressure of shareholders or the threat of raiders. While the resulting company would be loaded with debt, any profits would be distributed to a much smaller group of people, including the managers, providing enormous riches. The deals were rife with conflicts of interests, since managers had every incentive to sell the company to themselves on the cheap.

The peak of that buyout trend came in 1989, in the battle over

RJR Nabisco, recounted in detail in one of the great business books of the century, *Barbarians at the Gate,* by two men who were my colleagues at the *Wall Street Journal* at the time, Bryan Burrough and John Helyar.

The book is a remarkably detailed portrait of the state of corporate management at the end of the 1980s. Ross Johnson, the chief executive of RJR Nabisco, was a man wedded to the perquisites of unchallenged corporate power. To suit his own living preferences, he moved the company's headquarters from its birthplace in Winston-Salem, North Carolina, to Atlanta, Georgia, and decorated his offices there with Chinese antiques and French Empire mahogany chairs worth $30,000 apiece. An avid antique buyer, Johnson's office had thousands of dollars' worth of 18th-century porcelain china. A candy cart carrying French confections came through the office twice a day, and top managers were showered with complimentary country club memberships and luxury company cars. Johnson himself had company memberships in two dozen clubs and would golf with celebrities such as Arnold Palmer.

The most extravagant perquisite was the "RJR Air Force"—a fleet of private jets that shuttled Johnson and his celebrity friends anyplace they wanted to go. An RJR jet took football host Frank Gifford and his new bride Kathie Lee on their honeymoon. It shuttled ABC chieftan Roone Arledge on regular trips from Los Angeles to San Francisco. The planes were even dispatched when Johnson's dog, Rocco, bit a security guard at the Dinah Shore golf tournament in Palm Springs, and had to be flown quickly back East to escape retribution.

Johnson was also a master at ensuring the loyalty of his board, by showering them with rich contracts, contributions to their favorite charities, and perquisites. Former commerce secretary Juanita Kreps, for instance, was given $2 million to endow two chairs at Duke University, one of them named after her. Board member Bill

Anderson of NCR was given an $80,000 contract for his advisory services. Johnson disbanded RJR Nabisco's shareholder services department and contracted its work instead to director John Medlin's Wachovia bank. All of the directors were given access to the RJR Air Force anytime, anywhere.

All this served to put a thick layer of protection between Johnson and his shareholders. He could spend their money with abandon, and feel confident that the "shareholders' representatives"—the directors—would never take him on.

In the new corporate environment of the 1980s, Johnson still had to worry about raiders as a potential threat to his power. And the peculiar economics of tobacco made RJR Nabisco the perfect target for a raid. Because cigarettes were cheap to produce and addictive, the company was able to charge high prices and generate huge amounts of cash. But because tobacco was increasingly under attack for its health effects, the company was undervalued by shareholders. It was a classic opportunity for raiders to buy the company cheap, slash excessive costs, and reap the huge profits for their own benefit.

To help ward off such an attack, Johnson got the RJR Nabisco board to approve a set of antitakeover provisions. They included generous "golden parachutes"—severance agreements worth in total some $52.5 million that were placed in protective trusts and would be paid to Johnson and his closest allies in the event of a takeover.

Still, Johnson liked being on the cutting edge of business, and he realized a management buyout of RJR Nabisco would enable him to retain power and earn a fortune that went far beyond his current corporate pay package. So he joined forces with the investment bankers at Shearson Lehman Hutton and launched an effort to buy his own company, sparking one of the greatest business battles of the 20th century.

In the end, Johnson lost. His board lost faith in him, particularly after directors learned how generously he planned to compensate himself in the deal. The *New York Times* ran a story detailing the benefits he would receive and ran a headline saying "Nabisco Executives to Take Huge Gains in Their Buyout." *Time* magazine ran a cover story titled "A Game of Greed."

The company agreed to a $25 billion buyout by Kohlberg Kravis Roberts, which for the next two decades stood as the biggest buyout in history. It also marked the end of the buyout boom. The deal didn't turn out well. The junk bond market subsequently collapsed. And the maestro of junk bonds, Michael Milken, was sent to prison on insider-trading charges.

The collapse of the junk bond market and the widespread adoption of poison pills caused the raider movement to die down by the early 1990s. State court rulings also helped slow down the trend. The Delaware courts, long the friend of corporate managers, ruled in a critical 1989 case that Time Inc. could reject a hefty $200-per-share offer from Paramount Communications without putting the matter to a shareholder vote. "In the history of corporate governance, the Paramount decision is what Babe Ruth is to home runs," said Joseph A. Grundfest, a professor at Stanford Law School and former SEC commissioner. "The net result was to give corporate managements far greater discretion than many people think they ought to have."

5 |||||||||||||||||||||||||||||

The fight against the raiders cost corporate managers plenty in terms of the goodwill of other shareholders. The fact that CEOs were so willing to sacrifice shareholder interest in order to maintain control of their companies underscored the basic conflict of interest that Berle and Means had written about a half century earlier. The brazen power plays shocked some previously passive shareholders into action, and gave birth to a powerful new group of activists: public pension funds.

The rise of pension funds in the latter part of the 19th century added an important new element in the battle for corporate power. Berle and Means had written about how corporations had separated the owners of capital from the managers of capital. But pension funds brought another degree of separation into the game. The managers of giant companies were agents for the owners. Increasingly, the owners were large pension funds, who in turn were agents for the people whose retirement assets were at stake. In 1976, management guru Peter Drucker chronicled this new development and explored its deep implications in a book titled *The Unseen Revolution: How Pension Fund Socialism Came to America.*

Drucker was well ahead of his time. In 1970, individuals still held most U.S. stock, while institutions—pension funds, insurance companies, mutual funds, etc.—held only 15.8 percent. By 1981, the institutional share would increase to 38 percent, and by 1990, it would be 53 percent. Half of all the shares of U.S. corporations would end up in the hands of a relatively small number of financial institutions.

Traditionally conservative and passive investors, many pension funds simply "indexed" their holdings—or held a variety of stocks in predetermined portions. As the funds grew larger, the practice of selling off stocks that weren't performing well became increasingly difficult. If a large institution tried to sell off all its holdings in a single stock, it could drive down the price of that stock, forcing larger losses on itself as a result. Moreover, the only other buyers for such large blocks of shares were other institutions. As a result, it was difficult for pension funds to abandon stocks once they had taken a large position. "The economics of massive institutional ownership makes exit increasingly unattractive and prohibitively costly," wrote academic James P. Hawley.

With exits blocked, pension funds couldn't use the traditional means of exercising their shareholder "rights"—that is, selling stocks that they had lost confidence in. As a result, they had to pioneer a new way. They became activists, seeking to use their massive shareholdings as a club to influence corporate management and protect their investments.

Leading the charge was California treasurer Jesse Unruh. A big man—nearly 300 pounds—and a consummate political organizer, Unruh had become an important national figure during his days as the Democratic Speaker of the California Assembly in the 1960s. His size and his clout earned him the name "Big Daddy."

Unruh lost the race for governor to Ronald Reagan in 1970, but came back four years later to be elected treasurer. In that position, he had responsibility for the giant pension funds the state ran on behalf of its employees.

Like many investors, Unruh was outraged by the greenmail paid out by corporate managers in the 1980s. When Walt Disney paid a hefty premium to buy back Saul P. Steinberg's 11 percent equity stake, Unruh did a quick calculation. The Steinberg deal caused Disney stock to plunge 15 dollars. One of California's pension funds held 500,000 shares of Disney, which meant it took a hit of $7.5 million. That followed the Bass brothers' successful attempt to get a buyout from Texaco, a company in which California funds owned 1.4 million shares—roughly 1 percent of the total Texaco shares outstanding. The upshot of all this was clear to him: In their desperate efforts to hold on to power, corporate managers at Disney and Texaco were in effect stealing from California pensioners.

Unruh started working the phones, and in short order had put together a coalition of state pension funds, including those from Wisconsin, New Jersey, Connecticut and New York. They formed the Council of Institutional Investors. With 22 funds and collective assets of more than $100 billion, they were a powerful new force on the corporate scene.

The council's existence reflected a sea change in the ownership of equities in the United States that occurred between 1970 and 1990. Pension funds had become big players, and were now organizing to show that clout. A sleeping giant had been awakened— much to the dismay of corporate managers. "If these institutions start speaking with one voice," warned Ken Miller, head of Merrill Lynch's merger and acquisition group, "they could become a financial OPEC."

The combined force of these funds started to have some effect, using shareholder resolutions as a way of expressing their views. Few of their shareholder proposals were actually adopted. In 1991, for instance, 153 shareholder proposals were presented to U.S. corporations, of which 101 came to a vote and only eight won a plurality of the votes cast. Perhaps more telling of the pension funds' new clout was the fact that 20 proposals were withdrawn because management negotiated concessions prior to the annual meeting. In many of these cases, the pension funds got companies to abandon poison pill proposals or golden parachutes.

In an article in the *Harvard Business Review* in March–April 1991, Peter Drucker, who had been one of the first to spot the pension fund trend, noted that the 20 largest pension funds (13 of them funds for state, municipal or nonprofit employees) now held about one-tenth of all the equity capital of American publicly owned companies. The rise of these pension funds as the dominant owners and lenders, he said, "represents one of the most startling power shifts in economic history."

Dale Hanson, the chief executive of the California Public Employees' Retirement System, felt the shift as it was taking place. In the fall of 1989, Hanson wrote General Motors chief executive Roger Smith and asked for a meeting. Smith, without consulting the board, told the fund to mind its own business. Later that year, when Hanson wrote Smith's successor, Robert C. Stempel, to request a meeting, the company's general counsel Harry Pearce called back asking when. By November 1992, when John F. Smith replaced Stempel, Hanson didn't need to write. Pearce invited Hanson to visit Smith.

As a result, delivering returns to shareholders became the new watchword of American corporations. In 1950, Ralph Cordiner, CEO of General Electric, had asserted that top management in large, publicly owned corporations needed to manage their enterprises "in the best-balanced interests of shareholders, customers, employees, suppliers and plant community cities." But shareholders clearly wanted to be more than just one in a long list.

Another critical player in the rise of pension fund power was Robert A. G. Monks. A Harvard-educated lawyer, Monks ran the family-owned coal-and-oil business before becoming chairman of a Boston investment firm. He became a leading Republican fundraiser and tried on several occasions, but failed, to win a seat in the U.S. Senate from Maine. He was a firmly established member of the East Coast WASP establishment, and an unlikely man to become a corporate revolutionary.

It was while he served as chairman of the Boston Company in the late 1970s that Monks began to understand the implications of the rise in pension funds and other institutional investors for corporate capitalism. In a 1979 letter to Derek Bok, then president of Harvard, he called on the university to become a more activist shareholder.

> Is there literally no one responsible for the ethical conduct of corporations? . . . It is part of our tradition that owners of property are required to maintain it so as not to become a nuisance to others; why, other than convenience, should the ownership of common stock be otherwise regarded?
>
> Is it right for a shareholder to complain of his own inability to affect the corporation and at the same time be allowed to keep the benefits from that of which he disapproves. Shouldn't a shareholder have the affirmative burden to urge standards of corporate citizenship on his management?

Because of his interest in pension funds, Monks was offered the opportunity during the administration of Ronald Reagan to join the Department of Labor and oversee ERISA—the Employee Retirement Income Security Act—which governed the behavior of pension funds. Monks accepted the job, declined the salary, and used the position to push his activist agenda. His goal: to make institutional investors play an active role overseeing the activities of the companies in which they invested. In a speech to the managers of a number of corporate pension funds at the Harvard Club, Monks laid down the essence of his philosophy:

> The fact is, you control a lot of assets, and if you don't understand that you have that power, you will be ceding it to

*other people. And if you don't use that power, you are en-
couraging abuse.*

As head of ERISA, Monks prodded pension funds to view oversight of corporations as part of their fiduciary duty. It was after leaving government, however, that he made his greatest contribution:
the creation of Institutional Investor Services, later known as Institutional Shareholder Services. The firm would help big institutional
investors evaluate corporate proxies and advise them how to vote.
ISS stood by to condemn managers who attempted to adopt golden
parachutes, poison pills, and other measures that stood in the way of
letting shareholders reap full value in their investment. And over
time, it became one of the most important players in the boardroom
revolts that were about to occur.

By 1997, the business community was ready to acknowledge the
inevitable. The Business Roundtable issued a report on September
10 that set the new standard for corporate dealings with institutional
shareholders. The report acknowledged that the "paramount duty"
of management and the board is to shareholders—more than to employees, customers, suppliers or the community. And it urged that
boards be composed of a "substantial majority" of outside directors,
who should meet at least once a year without the CEO or other insiders present.

Shareholder activist Nell Minow, who had helped Monks set up
ISS, crowed: "I'm not on the fringe anymore."

6 ||||||||||||||||||||||||||||||||

Firing a CEO is the ultimate act of corporate governance. But during the heyday of big American corporations—in the 1960s, 1970s and 1980s—it was an exceedingly rare event.

Any CEO worth the pay knew how to prevent internal threats, by keeping his "bosses"—the board of directors—in check. To begin with, boards were filled with members of the company's management team, who owed their jobs to the chief executive. Outside directors were chosen by the CEO himself, and were often the CEOs of other companies who obeyed the directors' golden rule: do unto other CEOs as you would have them do unto you. Because the chief executive was also chairman, he controlled the board agenda and the flow of information to the board.

The only real threats to the power of a chief executive came from the outside—from another company launching a hostile takeover, or from raiders like Icahn or Pickens. The threat from inside—a rebellious board—was virtually nonexistent.

Until 1992. That was the year that the General Motors board, like Rip van Winkle, awoke from a 20-year slumber.

At the time, the world's largest car company was a mess. Its market share had been falling steadily, thanks to an onslaught of Japanese cars that were, simply and undeniably, better made than anything GM had to offer. Led by Toyota, the Japanese companies were far more efficient than their American counterparts, and their cars were far more reliable. All of Detroit was slow to rise to the challenge, but the lumbering giant, GM, was slowest. It was trapped in an insular culture that seemed impervious to change. Its cars were consistently at the bottom of lists ranking vehicles by quality and frequency of repairs. And by any conceivable measures—hours per car, workers per factory, dollars per car—it was the most inefficient company in the industry. Despite massive investments in automation in the 1980s, a GM car still took 30 to 35 hours of labor to assemble; Ford needed just 20 to 25.

On February 24, 1992, GM's chief executive and chairman Robert Stempel summoned reporters to the company's press room for a news conference. The company, he reported, was hemorrhaging money—a $4.45 billion after-tax loss in the previous year, including a $2.82 billion charge, shuttering plants and other restructuring costs.

Stempel attempted to put the best face on it, saying that minus the restructuring charge, the company's fourth quarter loss had been only a half-billion dollars, compared with $1.5 billion a year earlier. But his optimism rang hollow.

No GM chief executive had left against his will since 1920, when the company's founder William Crapo Durant was pushed out for speculating in the company's stock. Durant's board of directors had consisted of the people who were financing the company. J.P. Morgan and Company controlled six seats on the board. Pierre du Pont and the man he had installed as GM's treasurer, John Raskob, controlled two others. In those days, the owners were sitting at the table, and their tolerance for Billy Durant's financial shenanigans was limited.

All that had changed by 1992. Many of the men around the directors table were GM managers. These inside directors all sat on the same side of the board table, while the outside directors—most of whom knew little about the car business—sat on the other. Management directors were given different notebooks at each meeting, containing more information and backup than was provided to the outside directors. Board meetings tended to consist of upbeat slide shows that left all but the hardiest half asleep.

Still, the GM board in 1992 had two things going for it. One was an energetic Canadian named John G. Smale. He had risen through the ranks of Procter & Gamble to become chief executive in 1981, and had used his time there to shake up the consumer products giant. By the time he retired in 1990, P&G was bigger and more profitable than ever before.

The other was Ira Millstein, senior partner in the prestigious New York firm of Weil, Gotshal & Manges, who in his later years had turned himself into an expert, and something of a crusader, on matters of corporate governance. Millstein had started advising the GM board during the 1980s, when the company went through its ill-fated marriage and divorce with Ross Perot and his technology company, Electronic Data Systems. He began sharing his ideas about how boards should run—a far cry from the way they actually did. When Stempel's predecessor, Roger Smith, had tried to put three more GM officers on the board, directors, prodded by Millstein, had refused. On another occasion, Smith stormed up to Millstein's office—which happened to be on the 32nd floor of the GM building—after hearing he had had breakfast with a director at the Plaza Hotel. Talking to directors outside board meetings, Smith contended, was an unforgivable violation of the unstated board rules that existed at the time.

Gradually, GM's board members began to take Millstein's lessons to heart. On Sunday, January 5, 1992, Millstein assembled a group of outside directors on the phone to talk before the day's board meeting began. He told the directors about the "heightened duties of oversight" that fall on boards of troubled companies. They agreed to have a private meeting of just outside directors that night, instead of the presentation that Stempel had planned for them. In that meeting, they adopted a resolution saying John Smale had been designated to act on their behalf, and develop more information on the company's problems.

Smale spent the following month delving into GM's affairs, reading internal reports and outside data on GM's quality and productivity problems, and holding private conversations with top officials. What he found, and reported back to the board, was deeply disturbing. Even Stempel's top executives had little confidence that his plan for turning the auto giant around would work.

In March, the board demanded Stempel put in a new president, Jack Smith, and dump his handpicked man, Lloyd Reuss. From that point on, relations between Stempel and the board deteriorated. The board viewed Smith as an energetic change agent, while Stempel was seen as sulking and resisting the board's interference. Rumors that Smale, not Stempel, was really running GM became rampant in the press. On October 22, Stempel demanded that Smale put out a statement denying the rumors. Instead, the statement from Smale read as follows:

> The GM Board of Directors has taken no action regarding any management changes at GM. However, the question of executive leadership is a primary concern to the Board of Directors of any company, and GM is no exception. The GM Board of Directors continues to carefully reflect on the wisest course for assuring the most effective leadership for the corporation.

Even Stempel could read between those lines. The next day, he faxed to Smale a proposed letter of resignation. By late afternoon, the board's independent directors agreed to accept it.

GM's action had a profound effect across corporate America, and seemed to prod slumbering directors at other troubled companies into action. Within a short time, boards terminated CEOs at American Express, IBM, Eastman Kodak and Westinghouse.

The firing at American Express was particularly instructive. The

CEO James Robinson was replaced by his handpicked successor, Harvey Golub, and allowed to remain in place as chairman. That caused the company's stock to drop, and prompted outrage from a number of institutional shareholders. At a hastily organized breakfast with Golub, that included representatives of 20 percent of the company's shareholders, they demanded Robinson's resignation. Barely 24 hours later, Robinson did resign.

In the spring of 1994, at Ira Millstein's urging, the GM board issued 28 guidelines designed to guide its work as an independent board. They included:

- Independent board leadership in the form of a nonexecutive chairman or a lead independent director

- Regular meetings of the independent directors without management present

- Governance structure and process determined by the independent directors

- Annual board self-evaluations

- Selection of board member candidates by the independent directors, with input from the CEO

BusinessWeek christened the document a Magna Carta for directors. It marked an important step toward reining in the dictatorial CEO, and resolving the conflict between owners and managers highlighted by Berle and Means.

But if the goal of the 1990s "corporate governance" movement was to prevent managers from trampling the interests of owners, it was about to fail—and fail spectacularly.

7

For six straight years during the roaring bull market of the late 1990s, Enron Corporation was named "America's Most Innovative Company."

That was a high honor for a company based in the stodgy gas pipeline business, and operating in an age of technology upstarts like Amazon.com and Yahoo! Yet Enron had somehow managed to transform itself into the ultimate New Economy company. It had shed most of its hard assets, and focused instead on creating new marketplaces, in everything from weather futures to broadband Internet service. The company's chief executive, Kenneth Lay, was treated as something of a god among CEOs. The company employed 21,000 people, and claimed revenues of $101 billion in its peak year of 2000, and huge profits.

But no one seemed to know exactly how the company made its money. Others longed to emulate its success, but were somewhat mystified by it. Enron was a black box—a very successful black box, but a black box nonetheless.

In retrospect, it's now clear that the company was a giant bet on a rising market. As long as its stock kept rising, the intricate accounting games it was playing paid off. But when Enron's stock peaked in August of 2000 at $90 a share and started to decline, the problems emerged.

At the core of the company's problems were a complicated series of accounting maneuvers, which looked like they were getting assets off the company's books but which in fact left Enron liable for continuing losses. Often, the deals were done with stock as the currency. So when the stock price fell, the company had to pay up.

The backdrop for the Enron debacle was the story of stock options, their use and their abuse.

Options originally became popular as a solution to the Berle and Means problem of the conflicting interests of owners and managers. Give managers a big swig of options, reformers argued, and suddenly their interests would be aligned with the shareholders'. If the stock price went up, managers and shareholders would share the spoils. If it didn't, neither would gain.

Actions by government fueled the trend. In 1993, at the urging of the Clinton administration, Congress put a limit of $1 million on executive compensation, but excluded options and other performance-based pay. Meanwhile, under pressure from Congress, accounting authorities ruled that options didn't have to be counted as an expense on a company's books, since their value at the time they were issued was difficult to determine.

That set the stage for an explosion in options. It was "free money" that didn't have to go on the company's books. And it provided a backdoor route for executives to get rich.

For technology start-ups, options became the preferred means of rewarding employees. These companies could save cash by paying low salaries, and luring people with a promise of great riches in the future. As long as the market was rising, that promise paid off—often in spades. At companies like America Online, secretaries who had hoarded their options from the company's early days turned into millionaires.

At big companies like Enron, however, options had exactly the opposite effect of the one intended. Instead of aligning the interests of shareholders and managers, options quickly grew into the means of looting shareholders to make managers rich. The company could issue its executives enormous batches of stock options without undercutting reported earnings. And rising earnings would fuel further increases in the stock price, allowing the executives to cash in.

Once the stock market started to fall, that Ponzi scheme quickly unraveled. On October 16, 2001, Enron disclosed it was taking a half-billion-dollar charge against earnings and a $1.2 billion reduction of shareholders' equity because it was revising its accounting for transactions with one of the so-called "special purpose entities" it had created to fictitiously take assets off the company's books. Shareholders fled, and by November 30 the company filed for bankruptcy. At the time, it was the biggest bankruptcy in U.S. history, and cost 4,000 employees their jobs.

The Enron collapse sparked national outrage. Enron employees were particularly incensed—they had been urged to put all their savings into Enron stock, and then were urged to hold on to the stock even as executives sold theirs. Ken Lay sold tens of millions of dollars' worth of his stock as the company was going down, although he insisted he only sold what was necessary to meet credit calls on stock purchases.

Prior to Enron's collapse, the Bush administration was seen as friendly toward business. But as national outrage grew, the White House quickly changed course. President Bush was friends with Ken Lay, referred to him as "Kenny Boy," and had even considered making him secretary of the treasury. But as Lay's name became synonymous with corporate scandal, Bush quickly abandoned his friend. The administration set out to "get tough" on corporate criminals. It was President Bush's Justice Department that committed what is now considered one of the greatest overreactions of the period—the prosecution of accounting firm Arthur Andersen.

Andersen had been Enron's accountant, and David Duncan of the Houston office had blessed some of the company's most egregious accounting gimmicks. Moreover, once the problems became public, the company began shredding documents related to the Enron case. On March 7, the Justice Department indicted not just Duncan, but the entire firm. The indictment was, in effect, a death sentence for the company. Accounting firms survive on their reputations, and Andersen couldn't go on under the cloud of this indictment. As a result, thousands of innocent Andersen employees lost their jobs.

In a press conference on March 14, Deputy Attorney General Lawrence Thompson was asked by a reporter whether the fast indictment was a death sentence for the firm. His bland response: "I'm confident that the team, the task force, as well as myself, considered all the appropriate charges in making the decision to seek the indictment that we announce today."

On June 15, 2002, Andersen was convicted of obstruction of justice. The firm surrendered its licenses, now worthless anyway, on August 31 of that year. Three years later, the Supreme Court unanimously overturned Andersen's conviction based on flawed jury instructions, which allowed the jury to convict the company without proving that the firm knew it had broken the law. But by then, it was far too late.

Still, with the public angry and the media in a feeding frenzy, swift action was the order of the day. Any chance that the furor over Enron would die down was eliminated as a quick succession of new corporate scandals erupted.

In June of 2002, WorldCom revealed it had massively overstated its earnings to the tune of billions of dollars, leading to an SEC investigation and ultimately bankruptcy on July 21. That same month, Adelphia Communications Corporation founder John J. Rigas was charged with what the Securities and Exchange Commission called "one of the most extensive financial frauds ever to take place at a public company"—and was eventually convicted. A few months later, in September of 2002, Dennis Kozlowksi and his chief financial officer were charged with looting Tyco of hundreds of millions of dollars—and eventually convicted of those charges.

Congress, which usually has only two operating speeds—stalemate and overreaction—went into the latter mode. In whirlwind legislative sessions in the first six months of 2002, it adopted the Sarbanes-Oxley Act—the most sweeping rewrite of the securities laws since the 1930s. Its provisions, among other things:

■ Mandated that the board audit committee consist solely of independent board members, and be responsible for hiring and overseeing auditors

■ Required executives to certify reports, with criminal penalties for reckless certification

■ Mandated new disclosures regarding a firm's internal controls

■ Created a new regulatory agency to oversee accounting

The New York Stock Exchange also bent to the hurricane-force political winds, and adopted new listing requirements for companies, echoing some of the principles set out by Ira Millstein barely a decade earlier. Among them:

■ Listed companies were required to have a majority of independent directors, and the definition of "independence" was tightened.

■ Nonmanagement directors were required to meet in regularly scheduled "executive sessions" without management present.

■ Boards were required to have compensation committees, governance committees, and audit committees made up entirely of independent board members.

When it was all over, the tumultuous events of 2002 had resulted in an entirely new rule book for public corporations. It was clear that the great success story of the 20th century—the American corporation—was going to be something very different in the 21st.

8

Granting stock options to executives is an innovation gone badly awry.

Options, which started trading in Chicago in the early 1970s, give their holder the right to buy a stock in the future at a set price. Their use by executives was championed by reformers who saw them as an answer to the problem Berle and Means identified 50 years earlier. Corporate owners and corporate managers had different interests. Give the managers large swaths of options, however, and suddenly those interests would be aligned. If the stock price went up, everyone would gain. If it didn't, no one would.

The options craze got a further ironic boost in 1993, when, at the urging of the Clinton administration, Congress put a limit of $1 million on tax-exempt executive salaries, but excluded options and other performance-based pay from the cap. Also boosting the growth of options was the fact that accounting authorities had decided a decade earlier they didn't have to be counted as an expense on a company's books, since their value at the time they were issued was difficult to determine. The two changes caused executive options to skyrocket. Options could be issued at no cost to the company, and create the opportunity for vast riches.

The actions were backed by well-intentioned people who thought the spread of options would help what ailed corporate America. Instead, the cure turned out to be worse than the disease.

Fueled by options, CEO pay shot into the stratosphere. For the first time, executives had the opportunity to be paid like entrepreneurs. They responded accordingly, focusing their attention on their companies' stock prices. The result was a period of what Federal Reserve Board chairman Alan Greenspan later called "infectious greed." It was not that executives were any greedier than they used to be, he explained. It was that their opportunities to satisfy that greed—with options—were greater than ever.

When the market collapsed and the corporate scandals erupted at the turn of the century, the horrible consequences of this orgy of greed became apparent. In the quest for an ever-rising stock price, which in turn meant ever-greater options riches, executives had adopted a wide array of accounting gimmicks designed to fool shareholders. Massive restatements in earnings revealed what had become a giant con game—with executives falsifying their accounting so that shareholders would keep bidding up stock prices and executives could reap new riches from options.

As this book has shown, the public anger that followed the corporate scandals resulted in dramatic changes in the corporate world. But the one thing that has remained surprisingly impervious to change is CEO pay.

While CEO jobs were much less secure in 2005 than ever before, they weren't less lucrative. Thanks to the magic of options, a growing group of executives were taking home in excess of $100 million a year. That meant that each day of the year, they were earning $300,000 or more—six times what the average American earned in an entire year. Among the elite:

- Richard Fairbank of Capital One Financial, whose credit card business brought him total compensation in 2005 of $249.27 million. The money came entirely from the exercise of options.

- Bruce Karatz, of homebuilder KB Home, had compensation of $155.9 million, again mostly from options.

- Henry R. Silverman, CEO of the travel and real estate company Cendant Corporation, took in $133.26 million, largely from options.

- Richard S. Fuld Jr., head of Lehman Brothers Holdings Inc., earned $104.4 million, three-quarters from options.

In some cases these incomprehensibly large paychecks mirrored large returns to shareholders. KB Home, for instance, provided shareholders a return of 61 percent in 2005.

In other cases, however, the swelling options were the result of stock growth that had long since ended. Cendant, for instance, had shareholder returns of negative 21 percent in the year Silverman took his windfall. The company subsequently split up because of poor performance.

In many cases, the link between soaring pay and performance seemed to have broken down entirely. The Corporate Library, which researches corporate governance issues, has created a "Hall of Shame" filled with executives whose pay was completely out of whack with their company's performance. Among the shamed:

- Home Depot CEO Bob Nardelli, who had earned more than $200 million over five years, the Corporate Library said, at a time when his company was losing ground to competitor Lowe's Companies

■ William McGuire, United Health's CEO, who had raked in some $1 billion during his tenure in office, before accounting problems hit his stock

■ Hank McKinnell of Pfizer, who left office in 2006 with some $200 million even though the company's stock price fell during his tenure as CEO

To be sure, the critics of CEO pay played a little fast and loose with statistics. In some cases—Fairbanks, for instance—they would calculate pay by counting the cash value of options earned over many years at the time they were cashed in. In other cases, they would use an estimate of the options' value at the time they were issued, which might, in the end, bear little relationship to their value when cashed in. Nardelli's eye-popping $250 million pay figure, for instance, included $140 million worth of options that were "under water"—in other words, they entitled Nardelli to buy stock at a price higher than the current market price of the stock.

Even allowing for such statistical games, however, the numbers were hard for people to stomach. Corporate critics calculated that top CEOs earned 475 times the pay of the average American worker. Corporate defenders criticized some of the assumptions behind that number, and came up with a calculation of just 179 times the pay of the average worker. Either way, it was a huge difference, and far bigger than it had been two decades earlier.

Several studies, including one by Xavier Gabaix at MIT and Augustin Landier at New York University, concluded that soaring CEO pay largely tracked the soaring market value of companies since 1980, and thus reflected the results of the greatest bull market in stocks in American history. There were two problems with that argument, however: (1) average workers had seen only modest gains in their pay during the same period, and (2) the bull market had ended, while the CEO pay splurge had not.

In part, the continuation of huge executive pay figures post-Enron reflected executives' exercising options they had earned in the wild days before Enron. The numbers, however, also exposed a flaw in the way boards determined pay levels. The most common practice was to have a compensation consultant survey the pay of other CEOs in the industry. Because those consultants often worked for the CEO, and were eager to bring in more business, they had every incentive to ensure that the comparison group they used included plenty of well-paid executives. The board would then be tempted to offer a pay package that was better than the industry average, since no company wanted a "below average" CEO. The result was a one-way escalator, with each CEO building on the gains of others.

Soaring pay was also the ironic result of another characteristic of the post-Enron period—CEO firings. Often, when boards dumped their CEOs, they found themselves without obvious internal candidates to take the fired executives' place. That led to an outside search. Bringing in talent from the outside proved especially costly, and kept the CEO pay escalator moving upward.

When Boeing fired Harry Stonecipher, for instance, the board decided James McNerney, the former GE executive heading 3M, was the best man to replace him. To dislodge him, the board had to start by agreeing to give him $25.3 million in Boeing stock to replace payouts due to him from 3M in the future. And it's not as if he had suffered at 3M—in his last six months, he took home almost $41 million, including $32.4 million that came from exercising 3M stock options.

Particularly outrageous were the payouts that often went to fired executives, often because clever lawyers had negotiated big severance payments in contracts negotiated years earlier. Carly Fiorina left with $21 million. Franklin Raines, who had earned $90 million as CEO of Fannie Mae during a period when it was found to be exaggerating its earnings, got another $19 million when he departed. Phil Purcell left Morgan Stanley with a "golden parachute" worth some $52 million. Even Morgan Stanley's brief-tenured copresident Stephen Crawford, a Purcell loyalist who was put in the job during Purcell's desperate final days, left six months later with a settlement worth $36 million.

Arranging a merger or a buyout also turned out to be another way for CEOs to line their own wallets. After Procter & Gamble's takeover of razor maker Gillette, CEO James Kilts received $164.5 million in severance pay and "change of control" payments. In the 1980s, corporate reformers worried that CEOs had an incentive to fight takeovers that might be good for shareholders because they feared losing their jobs. By 2005, as the Kilts case demonstrated, takeovers were just one more path to CEO riches.

All of this created widespread public outrage. Some CEOs liked to blame the media for shining such a harsh spotlight on CEO pay. They wondered why they were coming under attack, when no one questioned, say, Tiger Woods's paycheck of $80 million a year, or rock stars and movie stars earning in the same league.

The media's glare, however, was reflecting public outrage as much as it was feeding it. And the outrage didn't come just from labor unions, left-leaning activists, or others practicing the politics of envy. It came from investors—capitalists—who felt they were being ripped off. They were happy to pay top dollar for managers who were making them money—witness the exorbitant fees being paid hedge fund managers. They weren't so happy, however, to see nine-figure paychecks going to the CEOs of companies that hadn't made a dollar for shareholders in years.

The outrage deepened in 2006, when my colleagues at the *Wall Street Journal* unearthed another scam that contributed to swelling executive paychecks—the backdating of options. By examining the dates on which options were issued, researchers were able to show that many companies had "backdated" their option grants to hit a low point in the stock's price. That thwarted the whole purpose of stock option grants. They were supposed to be an incentive for executives to perform better in the future. There was no "incentive" resulting from backdating grants, since they were already in the money at the time the executive received them. That was just another way of lining an executive's pocket.

Many CEOs were slow to recognize it—perhaps they enjoyed the results a little too much—but by 2006, CEO pay had become the driving force behind the public's outrage with corporate leaders. Enron might be sliding into the past, but excessive CEO pay was still very much a part of the present.

Some changes had occurred. Stock options, for instance, now had to be counted as an expense and deducted from earnings at the time they were issued. Also, the Securities and Exchange Commission approved new rules in 2006 requiring companies to be more explicit in reporting total pay to top executives. And, corporate boards now were putting pay more clearly in the hands of independent directors, and those directors were increasingly hiring independent consultants to work with them—instead of consultants being hired by the company.

Still, it was far from clear that the changes went far enough to rein in out-of-control pay. With the public now focused on the issue, getting out of the pay hole was going to be a lot more difficult than getting into it had been.

Corporations, as I've argued throughout, need the support of the public to survive and thrive. As long as pay practices remain out of kilter, however, there is little hope they will get that support.

CHAPTER THREE
THE NEW ORDER

Everywhere it gave rise to a vague awareness that a new order was in the making and to equally vague hopes of changes and reforms. But nobody as yet had any idea what form these were to take.

—Alexis de Tocqueville, *The Old Regime and the French Revolution*

1

Pattie Dunn says she never asked to become chairman of the board of Hewlett-Packard, and never particularly wanted the job.

The reason the directors asked her to take it on, she believes, is that they were badly divided, and she was one of the few people—perhaps the only person—still talking to those on both sides of the divide. She was the person who had carefully negotiated the 500-word statement of the board's common complaints that the three directors took to Fiorina in January 2005. She had insisted that the board pay close attention to proper process and procedure in its firing of Fiorina. She had thought a lot about corporate governance and talked a lot about corporate governance.

Moreover, she was a woman. Some of the directors realized that appointing a female chairman might soften the public relations blow that would inevitably follow from firing Fiorina, who had been celebrated as "the most powerful woman in business."

Fiorina herself suggests a more cynical explanation for Dunn's rise. She believes two other directors, Jay Keyworth and Tom Perkins, made an implicit, if not explicit, deal: If Dunn would support their effort to oust the CEO, she could become chairman.

There is little evidence to support Fiorina's belief. But there's ample evidence that while Keyworth and Perkins supported Dunn's elevation to chaiman, they paid her scant respect, either before or after she took the job.

In her book, *Tough Choices*, Fiorina says that Keyworth "had been derisive of Pattie Dunn's capabilities ever since I'd known him.

He routinely complained that she didn't understand the company and relied on process as a crutch. He'd frequently urged me to replace her."

After she became chairman, Perkins was more openly critical. He soon took to reminding her that he had been on the boards of more than a dozen venture capital companies simultaneously, and knew more about corporate governance than she could shake a stick at.

In more heated moments, he would poke his finger into her clavicle and shout, "I made you chairman. I got you an extra $100,000." Another director referred to Perkins's performances as "chairman abuse." After repeated references to her pay, Dunn felt compelled to sit down with Perkins and go over her own finances, so he would understand that she, like he, was not in need of the money.

Perkins and Dunn argued over things large and small. In the search for new directors for the board, he looked to other technology experts—suggesting three people who ran firms that had been financed by Kleiner Perkins. She looked to people with operational experience in big companies, and felt Perkins was merely trying to find directors who would solidify his influence on the board. He dismissed her nominees as "ciphers" from "large cap" companies.

They clashed later when Perkins published his first novel, a steamy romance fashioned after the work of his ex-wife, Danielle Steel, entitled *Sex and the Single Zillionaire*. The idea came from a television producer who once had asked him to participate in a reality show based on the premise of picking a new spouse. He declined, but made that the plotline for his book.

Perkins suggested that Hewlett-Packard sell the book on its Web site. Dunn rejected the request, saying it would be highly inappropriate. On another occasion, Perkins asked Dunn, in front of several top HP managers, whether she had read his book.

"I've only skimmed it," she replied.

"Oh come on," he said. "Even if you've just skimmed it, surely you've got an opinion."

"It's not really my thing."

Again he took her aside and started poking her in the collarbone. "Don't ever humiliate me in front of HP managers that way," he lectured her.

At the root of their fights was a fundamental disagreement about how large companies should be run. As a pioneer of the venture capital world, Perkins thought big companies needed to be more like the small companies he had helped start. In the venture world, the people who provide the money—i.e., people like Tom Perkins—had clout in proportion to their invested cash. They didn't worry about a vast army of unrepresented owners, or waste a lot of time on procedures and process. The venture capitalists were the owners, and they aggressively looked after their own interests.

Pattie Dunn, however, came from a very different world. The investment firm she once headed, Barclays Global Investors, ran $1.2 trillion in investment funds, earning it a place near the top of the list of largest shareholders for virtually every big company in the United States. She thought a lot about her company's fiduciary responsibilities to the investors in those funds, and its responsibilities as the nominal owner of such vast quantities of corporate stock. She took those responsibilities very seriously.

In an interview in the spring of 2006, before the investigation of boardroom leaks had exploded into a public scandal, Pattie Dunn told me that boards "are like the U.S. Senate. Everybody is important. Everybody has to have an opinion. You have to convince other people, and you have to have an ability to be convinced." She said that as chairman, she "spent 25 percent of my time telling everybody what everybody else thinks. I make sure the processes involve every director. That's my role."

Dunn argued that the evolution of power at Hewlett-Packard was an inevitable consequence of what she called "the democratization of wealth." As more and more people participate in the ownership of capital, those people inevitably want a say. "It's a necessary broadening of the power structure," she said. "Generally speaking, this is a good thing. It's something we need more of. I'm all for it. It's a good thing more people have a stake in capitalism."

Yet whether the democratization of corporate power would enable those corporations to continue their extraordinary 20th-century record of wealth creation, she added, is another matter. In the new structure, public companies have become "more focused on risk than returns." Would this new structure lead to superior—or even satisfactory—returns? That, she said, "is an open question."

Dunn had an unusual background for someone assuming such a prominent position in the corporate world. Her mother had been a showgirl in Philadelphia, and held political views that Dunn's husband later described as "left of Lenin." Her father was a vaudevillian, and became a union organizer for show business workers. The two met after Dunn's mother, dressed as the Statue of Liberty, fell down the steps during one of her shows. She was fired on the spot, but Dunn's father stepped in to defend her. Although he was 25 years her senior, they married, and moved to the only logical place for such a pair: Las Vegas.

For Dunn, that led to an unorthodox upbringing. Her father was entertainment director at Las Vegas hotels including the Dunes and the Tropicana. She recalled setting up a table at the casinos and selling Girl Scout cookies. "We sold thousands," she said. Guests at the family dinner table included Las Vegas regulars such as Lena Horne, Sammy Davis Jr., Dean Martin and Jimmy Durante.

She attended Catholic schools, and says that in some ways her upbringing was surprisingly conservative. "We were always in church," she recalled, "Our Lady of Las Vegas." Yet the mothers driving carpool were often showgirls, dressed for their next performance.

Dunn's father died when she was just 11, and her mother moved the family to Terra Linda, California. Cash was tight. She won a National Merit Scholarship in 1970 to go to the University of Oregon but had to drop out when her mother lost Social Security death benefits. For a year, Dunn worked days as an apartment rental agent and evenings cooking and housecleaning for a family in return for room and board. Her mother was homeless and slept in her car for a while.

In 1973, Dunn got enough scholarship and grant money to return to college at the University of California, Berkeley, as a journalism major. She dreamed of becoming a writer, and devoured the works of a new generation of authors like Truman Capote and Tom Wolfe. After Richard Nixon resigned in 1974, she, like thousands of other young, aspiring writers, hoped to become the next Bob Woodward or Carl Bernstein, the *Washington Post* reporters who uncovered the Watergate scandal.

She did not envision herself becoming a corporate leader. And she certainly never thought of working in finance. "I'd rather drink chloroform and die than work for a bank," she recalled.

In December of 1975, Dunn graduated from college and needed a job. So she took what was available: a temporary position at Wells Fargo Investment Advisers.

While she didn't know it at the time, she had joined an organization that was at the very forefront of an investment revolution. Wells Fargo was trying to take a stodgy and tradition-laden craft—money management—and turn it into a science. The firm was following the developments of academics like Fischer Black at the University of Chicago, and his colleagues Robert Merton and Myron Scholes, who had won the Nobel Prize for their development of mathematical models to explain the pricing of financial assets; and William Sharpe at nearby Stanford University, another Nobel winner in economics. The firm pioneered index investing—investing in a fixed basket of securities that matched one of the market indexes, like the Dow Jones average or the S&P 500.

Shortly after she arrived, Wells Fargo also began pioneering work in quantitative strategies of investment—investment using carefully calculated computer models rather than relying on gut human judgments. Later, the company pioneered exchange-traded funds, which made it easier for investors to buy a broad and diversified basket of stocks without paying high fees to a money manager.

In each of these investment approaches, Barclays was required to take custody of the stock, rather than pass ownership onto the ultimate beneficiary, as traditional money managers would do. As a result, Barclays became one of the biggest shareholders of record at most of the nation's largest companies.

Because she was a writer and they were not, the leaders of Barclays often turned to Dunn to help them express their steadily evolving views on investment. "I did what they asked me to do, and I understood what they were trying to accomplish," she said. Over time, as she learned their views, she "drank the Kool-Aid." She worked hard, moved up the ladder, and became president in 1994—a year before the firm was bought by Barclays Bank of the United Kingdom in 1995—then became cochairman in 1996, and finally chief executive of the investment firm in 1998, reporting directly to the CEO of Barclays Bank.

By pioneering indexing and quantitative investment strategies, Barclays was also putting itself at the center of the paradox that was challenging the 20th-century model of the corporation. In earlier days, investment managers helped impose discipline on companies by selling the shares of those they thought were going astray. But an index fund designed to hold all the stocks in, say, the

S&P 500 couldn't just dump a stock because the manager thought its company's management was being reckless, or overpaying its executives, or otherwise making mistakes. Who, then, was supposed to keep tabs on corporate managers, and check their power? How would the system prevent the abuses that inevitably happen when powerful people are left largely unaccountable?

Unlike activist pension funds like CalPERS, Barclays had been reluctant to take on the role of disciplinarian itself. After all, many of the companies it invested in were also its clients—corporations that invested their pension fund assets with Barclays. As a result, it tended to be a quiet investor. "We just wanted to manage money," says Dunn, "not get involved in running companies." Yet Barclays' innovations were undermining the checks and balances in the system of corporate power, nonetheless.

Recognizing the problem, Dunn pushed Barclays' quantitative wizards to try to find measures of corporate governance that would be associated with better corporate returns. Perhaps, she thought, the computer models could be designed to detect companies whose management was heading for trouble. Despite her urgings, however, the Barclays' researchers were unable to find any clear connection between good governance and good performance for shareholders.

In 1998, Dunn got a call from a headhunter who said she had been identified as a potential board member for Hewlett-Packard. Lewis Platt, then the CEO of the firm, was looking to bring more outsiders onto the board, which had traditionally been dominated by members of the Hewlett and Packard families, and by managers at the firm. Platt had recruited Boeing CEO Phil Condit—a move that led to his later intricate involvement with Boeing—and also Sam Ginn, the chief executive of AirTouch Communications.

It was an unusual offer. For the most part, money managers do not sit on large corporate boards. There's an inherent conflict. Would the manager be more inclined to invest funds in a company because of a board seat? Or would that seat perhaps provide an insight into company affairs that other managers don't share?

Dunn's bosses at Barclays Global Investors were concerned. But Dunn pleaded with them. Hewlett-Packard was one of the best-known technology companies in the world, with a storybook history that began with its founding in the garage of two Silicon Valley legends. Technology was hot in 1998, and Dunn wanted to be a part of it. So her bosses agreed.

Dunn didn't know it, but she was joining the HP board at the beginning of a whirlwind of change. At one of her first meetings, Lew Platt, the man who had recruited her, stood up and told the board he had concluded he was not the right man for the top job. He had been under intense pressure from board members like Hackborn, but he chose to portray his resignation as his own decision. A nationwide search for a replacement was launched, and the search committee picked Carly Fiorina—without ever even introducing her to the full board. The first time Dunn even met her was at Fiorina's first board meeting.

Still, Dunn, like the others, was taken in by Fiorina's charisma and charm. "This was a company that needed invigorating," she said. "Fiorina was smart, energetic. I was a big supporter." She stood firmly behind Fiorina as the CEO sought board approval for the massive merger with Compaq, and stood with her in the bruising battle against Walter Hewlett to win shareholder approval for that merger.

In 2002, however, Dunn's life took a dramatic turn. She was diagnosed with breast cancer and melanoma. She stepped down from the top job at BGI to become nonexecutive chairman. Yet Dunn didn't give up her seat on the Hewlett-Packard board, and her role on the board increased even as she was struggling with chemotherapy.

2

When the Hewlett-Packard board asked Dunn to become nonexecutive chairman in February of 2005, they were taking an unusual step for an American company. The post was favored by many corporate reformers, but was still a rarity at American companies. A report by Spencer Stuart, the recruiting firm, found that in 2005, only 30 percent of companies in the S&P 500 had a separate chairman and CEO. At most of those, the chairman's seat was filled either by an ex-CEO who had been kicked upstairs, or by another person closely connected with the management of the company. Only about 9 percent of S&P 500 companies had a chairman who could be considered truly independent—that is, a chairman like the one Pattie Dunn had been asked to become.

The board discussed making Dunn's appointment temporary, in case a new CEO demanded the chairman's title as well. In the end, however, directors feared a temporary appointment would only add to the sense that the company was leaderless. If a candidate for the CEO position insisted on being chairman, they figured, they could deal with that when it happened.

As the new chairman, of course, her first job was to find a new chief executive. She decided the entire board should be involved in the search—not just a small committee like the one that had found Fiorina. Together, they worked with remarkable speed, and selected the man then heading the NCR Corporation, Mark Hurd. He, too, was the opposite of Fiorina—low-key, focused on operations, not interested in making speeches or becoming a global ambassador. At the time, he was also perfectly willing to let Dunn remain in the job of chairman. He knew the HP board was a fractious group, and was happy to let someone else worry about managing that group.

In addition to finding a new CEO, Dunn turned her attention to the operations of the board. In April and May of 2005, she visited each of the HP directors, usually at their homes, and talked with them for several hours about how they felt the board should be run. There was still a great deal of distrust and suspicion among the group. "I just thought: This is like the Arabs and Israelis," she recalls.

Many of the board members were still upset about the leak of the details of the January board meeting to the *Wall Street Journal*. Moreover, a subsequent leak to *BusinessWeek* about their efforts to recruit Mark Hurd deepened those concerns. Most felt it would be difficult to operate effectively as a board so long as they had to worry that their deliberations would appear in the press. In her private conversations, Dunn later said, seven of the nine directors emphasized that the leaks had to be stopped.

Keyworth was not one of the seven. He had another concern. Larry Babbio, the Verizon executive who headed the board's compensation committee, had approved a big bonus for Fiorina and her team in December, even as the board was airing its grievances with the CEO. Surely that was a sign of a governance problem, he thought.

As the deep divisions on the board became clearer to her, Dunn says, she thought about resigning. She talked to a governance expert, however, who advised strongly against it. She had a fiduciary duty to the shareholders to fix the problem.

So Dunn began her effort to remake the board. She would seek as many as four new members to build a new working majority. And she would carry out a deeper investigation of the leaks. At the time, she suspected Jay Keyworth as the culprit, as had Fiorina. But suspicions weren't enough. She would need proof before she could take action.

For help in carrying out the investigation, Dunn turned to Bob Wayman, the company's chief financial officer who, at the time, was filling in as acting chief executive until a new one came on board. He referred Dunn to Kevin Huska, the company's head of Global Security. Huska in turn told her to talk with Ron DeLia, who was an outside contractor who had implemented a number of investigations involving breaches of confidential information for HP. Dunn spoke with DeLia several times to discuss the investigation of the boardroom leak. At one point, DeLia told her it was customary for these investigations to have a name, and asked her what she would like to name this one. Dunn was vacationing in her home in Kona, Hawaii, at the time, so she said to call it "Kona."

What's unclear, in retrospect, is exactly how much Dunn knew about the tactics that would be used in this leak investigation. She certainly knew that it involved gathering the private phone records of directors and journalists. She later insisted, however, she had no understanding that it would involve "pretexting"—which meant investigators fraudulently pretended to be directors and journalists—and even used their Social Security numbers—in order to obtain records.

In interviews after the investigation blew up and became public, Ron DeLia, the consultant who headed the investigation, said he had no doubt he discussed the methodology of pretexting with Dunn at some point during the 2005 investigation. In particular, he recalled a June 15, 2005, conference call with Dunn and HP general counsel Ann Baskins in which he went over the results of the investigation to date, including third-party phone records. During the call, he said, he explained pretexting, telling Dunn and Baskins it involved investigators pretending to be someone else in order to get information from the telephone company. Handwritten notes taken by Baskins during the call confirm that Dunn participated, and that pretexting was discussed.

Dunn, however, claimed in later interviews that she had no recollection of ever hearing the word "pretexting" until long after the investigation was finished in 2006. She did not recall the June 14 conference call with DeLia and Baskins, according to investigators, "though she stated it was entirely possible that such a call occurred, and that the participants may have discussed phone pretexting."

When asked later at the congressional hearing how she thought investigators were obtaining private phone records, Dunn replied: "My understanding was these records were publicly available."

"So you think I can call up, as anybody in the public, and get your phone records?" asked an incredulous Greg Walden, Republican from Oregon.

"I thought a year ago, I thought six months ago, that you could," Dunn said.

"You really believe that?" asked Walden. "You honestly thought it was that simple?"

"Yes," Dunn replied.

The investigation went on for several months, and involved tactics that went well beyond the use of phone records. After the investigation became public, my colleague Pui-Wing Tam, who had written the explosive January 2005 story that had started it all, was allowed to see some of the information the company collected on her during its investigation. In addition to trying—and succeeding—on multiple occasions to obtain her telephone records, they also rifled through the trash at her suburban home. Investigators reviewed videotapes of Tam, and would stake out events attended by directors to see if she would show.

"H-P built up information on my husband, including where we got engaged and married," Tam wrote in a *Journal* story in October. "H-P sleuths reviewed voicemails I'd left for an H-P director, and got a description of my car. They read my instant messages to an H-P media-relations executive. According to the California attorney general, H-P's investigators also used the last four digits of my Social Security number to impersonate me in order to obtain my phone records." In short, it was clear the investigation led to some shocking invasions of people's privacy.

By August of 2005, the investigators had little to show for their efforts. They had narrowed the list of suspects, but were unable to develop conclusive evidence that any one member of the board, or of the company's executive team, was responsible for the leaks. Dunn said she regularly informed the board of the investigation, but provided few details, at the investigators' request. In August, Project Kona came to an inconclusive end.

In January of 2006, however, the board again held its annual off-site meeting with HP management, this time at the Esmeralda Resort and Spa, near Palm Springs, California. It had been exactly one year since the meeting in San Francisco, when directors had their showdown with Fiorina. And this time, just as a year earlier, within days details of the meeting found their way to the press.

CNET News, a technology-news Web site, ran a story with details from the private meeting, quoting a "source with the company." Some of the information provided by the source was mundane. "By the time the lectures were done at 10 p.m., we were pooped and went to bed," the story quoted the source saying. But some got to the core of the company's plans. The source said HP might buy more software companies and might work more closely with chip maker Advanced Micro Devices as "a cattle prod of sorts" to HP's long-standing chip supplier, Intel.

Dunn was appalled, as was chief executive Mark Hurd, and together they launched Kona II. Dunn suggested to general counsel Ann Baskins that she hire Kroll Associates to conduct this investigation, but Baskins instead turned the investigation over to Kevin

Hunsaker, who again retained Ron DeLia. This time, because the information in the CNET story was so specific, investigators were able to narrow the likely sources, and began to focus in on Keyworth. They tried a number of unorthodox tactics—tailing Keyworth to see if he met with the CNET reporter, sending a fake e-mail concerning company business with a "tracer" attached to it to the reporter to see who she forwarded it to. In the end, they were able to obtain phone records showing Keyworth had talked on the phone with the CNET reporter around the time the stories ran. Moreover, there was evidence that seemed to link Keyworth to other leaks—although not the key story in the *Wall Street Journal* that had provoked the confrontation with Fiorina.

Before the regularly scheduled board meeting on May 18, Dunn and Ann Baskins, the company's general counsel, decided to give the report on the investigation to Robert Ryan, head of the board's Audit Committee and former chief financial officer of Medtronic Inc. Dunn and Baskins concluded the leak was a violation of the company's Standards of Business Conduct, which are overseen by that committee. In doing so, they bypassed the Nominating and Governance Committee, then headed by Perkins, which normally handled matters concerning board operations. Perkins had become an annoyance to both Dunn and Hurd, and he was a close friend and ally of Keyworth. Moreover, he was insistent that if a leaker was identified, the problem should be handled in private, and not brought before the entire board. Dunn felt she had a responsibility to share the results with the full board.

Talking points prepared for Ryan traced the history of the "Kona II" investigation. The talking points included no mention of "pretexting." But they did note that private phone records had been obtained. A footnote said that the investigation team "utilized a lawful investigative methodology commonly utilized by entities such as law firms and licensed security firms in the United States to obtain such records."

The report concluded that George Keyworth "was the source who leaked non-public, confidential information" to CNET reporter Dawn Kawamoto in January, and "in conjunction with at least six other articles since March of 2002." The evidence against Keyworth "is extensive and multifaceted," the talking points said, and included phone records showing "telephonic contact between Kawamoto and Keyworth" before the January story.

On the day of the May 18 board meeting, Ryan met with Keyworth for breakfast at HP's headquarters and reviewed the findings of the investigation. Keyworth was shocked at the information in the report, and admitted to having had lunch with the CNET reporter. Knowing that Perkins and Keyworth were close, Ryan also pulled Perkins into a private room before the board meeting and briefed him on the report.

In the board meeting, Ryan went over the investigative report in detail. Keyworth was given a chance to explain himself. He apologized, but didn't seem to feel his conversations with reporters had hurt the company or been improper. He was then asked to leave the room, and the board had a long discussion. A turning point came when Hurd was asked by a director how he would handle the matter if it had been an employee who had talked to the reporter. Hurd replied, "I would have no choice but to fire him," according to a board member. A motion was made and seconded that Keyworth be asked to resign. Six members voted for the motion; three opposed.

As it became clear the board was going to ask Keyworth to resign, Perkins grew increasingly angry. Directors say he defended Keyworth as a valuable and long-standing director, and said a "good man" was being trashed by the process. He said that while he had supported Dunn's push for a leak investigation, he had argued the findings should not be reviewed in a full board meeting, but rather handled confidentially by the Nominating and Governance Committee, of which he was chairman. After the vote, he attacked Dunn, saying, "Pattie, you betrayed me. You and I had an agreement we would handle this offline without disclosing the name of the leaker." Dunn denied ever agreeing to Perkins's demand.

Finally, Perkins rose from his seat, slammed his briefcase shut, and said, "I quit and I'm leaving."

After a moment of silence, Ryan turned to Ann Baskins. "Ann, is that a bona fide resignation?" Baskins said if the board voted to accept the resignation, it would be valid. Ryan responded, "I so move." His motion was quickly seconded and adopted—a sign that, aside from Keyworth, most of the directors had lost patience with Perkins.

Dunn and Ryan then left the meeting to discuss the board's action with Keyworth. He refused to resign. The shareholders had elected him, he insisted, and he would stay on the board until the shareholders decided otherwise.

At 2:20 in the afternoon, the board recovened, without Keyworth or Perkins. The board then began a discussion of its responsibility to disclose the event. The law requires that when a director resigns, the company has to disclose whether it was the result of a fundamental disagreement.

Perkins was on his way to Turkey, to oversee the maiden voyage of *The Maltese Falcon*—a remarkable 290-foot clipper and one of the largest sailing yachts in the world. Contacted by Larry Sonsini, HP's outside counsel, about his reasons for leaving the board, Perkins reportedly said: "Just don't make it for personal reasons. I don't want people to speculate about my health." He previously had invited members of the board to come to Turkey for the launching of the *Maltese Falcon*, but after his resignation, he contacted Dunn's office to rescind her invitation.

Acting on Sonsini's advice, board members concluded that Perkins had no disagreement with the company, only with Dunn. Therefore, they decided they had no obligation to file details with the SEC. Instead, the board issued a statement on May 19 that said simply that

Perkins had resigned, effective immediately. In the statement, Hurd thanked Perkins for his service, and added, "He has been instrumental in championing improvements that are leading to a stronger H-P." As for Keyworth, the board agreed he would not be renominated as part of the 2007 directors slate.

3 ||||||||||||||||||||||||||||||

Tom Perkins was clearly angry. He was used to getting his way. But Pattie Dunn had gotten the best of him. Her investigation had humiliated his friend George Keyworth, and had prompted him to resign angrily from the Hewlett-Packard board. Directors say Perkins made an attempt to regain his seat, but it was too late.

So Perkins decided to go to war. He enlisted the help of a conservative lawyer, Viet Dinh, whom he had met through his seat on the News Corp board. Dinh felt confident that the "pretexting" used against him was illegal, and agreed to represent him in the matter. And with Dinh's help, he went on the warpath. His target, it was clear, was Pattie Dunn.

On June 19, Perkins sent the following e-mail to Sonsini:

Hi Larry:

Today I was at a NewsCorp board meeting in London, and I discussed the events of the most recent HP board meeting, on a confidential basis, with a fellow director, Viet Dinh. As you probably know, Viet is a Professor of Law

*at Georgetown, and his most popular course is "Corporate
Governance."*

*Viet was shocked at the HP chairman's recording of
board members' telephone and computer interconnections.
I emphasized that no communications were actually tran-
scribed. He said that even monitoring connections and/or
e-mail addresses requires a subpoena (which as far as I
know was never obtained) but, with or with e out [sic] a
subpoena, such monitoring was simply "unconscionable."*

Larry, was any of this cleared with you before the event?

Thanks in advance for your thoughts.

Best, Tom

Within an hour, Sonsini had responded:

Tom,

*I was not involved in the design or conduct of the investi-
gation. The investigation was run by the HP legal department with outside experts. I reviewed the report after the
investigation for the Board process. Pattie was not involved
in the design or conduct of the investigation either, to my
knowledge. I am sure that Ann Baskin looked into the legality of every step of the inquiry and was satisfied that it was
conducted properly.*

Then came an effort to try to silence Perkins:

*Tom, be careful of your discussions about the inquiry and
the HP Board process and deliberations in that all of that is
confidential and, as you know, you have the obligation to
continue to respect that confidentiality. You do not want to
be in breach of your duties inherited while you were an HP
director. Those duties of confidentiality continue. Also, re-*

*member, that you confirmed that you did not have any dis-
agreement with HP or the Board as a whole (although you
did have issues with the Chairman). I recognize that a duty
of loyalty to the Newscorp Board may present some concerns for you, but in my opinion they do not, and should not.
[sic] require you to disclose the details of the investigation or
the HP Board deliberations. Also, Viet Dinh may be a lawyer
but query whether your discussions are attorney-client priv-
ileged. If you want to talk about all of this please don't hesi-
tate to call.*

Larry

The next day, Perkins replied:

Dear Larry:

*Thanks for your prompt reply, and I value the reminder
that my director's responsibilities continue after my resignation, which is why, in part, I make the following suggestion:
I think you, or someone from your firm, should check into
the sub-rosa investigation of the director's [sic] communications at HP. Larry, the investigation was a Pattie Dunn program, 100%—conceived and managed by her, and unknown
to the board, except perhaps in the most vague and impre-
cise terms, with the possible exception of Mark, who she
may have briefed.*

*In view of Viet's unqualified opinion that it was illegal,
I think, the board needs to know the potential risks, if any.
I resigned from the board and as chair of the N&G committee before I could look into this personally. If it was illegal, it
occurred under my purview, and on my watch, so to speak,
and I would like to know whether or not I share some responsibility.*

Thanks, Tom

Eight days later, on June 28, Sonsini came back with the following response, under a subject line: *"HP Confidential."*

> *Tom,*
>
> *I looked into the conduct of the investigation and got a report from counsel at HP who was responsible for the effort. I confirmed his input by talking to Ann Baskins. Here is what I learned:*
>
> 1. *There was no recording, review or monitoring of director e-mail.*
> 2. *There was no electronic surveillance to monitor director communications.*
> 3. *There was no phone recording or eavesdropping.*
> 4. *The investigating team did not attempt to obtain the phone records of non-employee directors.*
> 5. *The investigating team did obtain information regarding phone calls made and received by the cell or home phones of directors. This was done through a third party that made pretext calls to phone service providers. Apparently a common investigatory method which was confirmed with experts. The legal team also checked with outside counsel as to the legality of this methodology.*
> 6. *There was no "secret spying" i.e. no electronic gear, listening devices, etc., were used. [sic]*
>
> *It appears, therefore, that the process was well done and within legal limits. The concerns raised in your e-mail did not occur.*
>
> *Let me know if you think I should proceed further.*
>
> *Larry*

Sonsini, who is almost as much of a fixture in Silicon Valley as Perkins, must certainly now regret these e-mails. In a phone conversation with me months later, he denied that his firm had verified the legality of the "pretexting" technique. Indeed, the technique seems to be patently illegal in many states, if not under federal law. In subsequent testimony before Congress, Sonsini said he wrote his e-mail to Perkins before doing his own investigation of the matter, and relied on assurances from Baskins that the investigative tactics were legal.

Perkins had all he needed to launch his jihad. He contacted the Securities and Exchange Commission, to argue that the HP board had inaccurately stated the reasons for his resignation. He contacted the California attorney general, who began investigating the matter.

He also contacted AT&T, and received a letter in return on August 11 confirming that his personal phone had been subject to "pretexting." The letter in response, from a Travis Dodd, said that someone using his name had established an online account on January 30, 2006, and accessed the account on that day. The letter went on to say:

> Notably, that appears to be the only date of access to this account—i.e. it appears this was a one-time attempt to obtain information and although your billing records for December 2005 and January 2006 would have been accessible, it appears that the person reviewed only your bill for the January 2006 billing period. The person registering the online account did so through the Internet and provided your telephone number and the last four digits of your Social Security Number to identify himself/herself as the authorized account holder. We have no way of determining how the person obtained this Social Security Number information.

The letter said someone attempted to open an online account for his AT&T long-distance account, on January 29, 2006. The initial attempt to do so over the Internet failed. So the person called the AT&T Customer Care Unit, represented himself as Perkins, provided identifying information to the service representative, and then opened the account. That account was accessed on February 2, 2006.

In both cases, it's clear, the investigators were trying to find if Perkins had talked with the CNET reporter who wrote the January story.

Perkins then penned a letter to the HP board, claiming the company had misrepresented his resignation in its report to the SEC, and that its investigation had likely violated the law. He put the company on notice.

The dispute between Perkins and HP remained out of the press through most of the summer. But Perkins told an ever-widening group of people.

I first heard of Perkins's battle in late August, and began to report on the troubled May meeting of the Hewlett-Packard board. In early September, I wrote the details of the board's showdown in my "Business" column for the *Wall Street Journal*. The same day, the company filed an amended account of its May board meeting, with many of the details of the board battle, with the Securities and Exchange Commission. The reports quickly turned into a national scandal, with *Newsweek* running a cover story on Dunn entitled "The Boss Who Spied on Her Board."

In an early statement on the matter, Dunn tried to minimize the brouhaha as "part of the board's progression from one that was more personality driven to one that is process driven and capable of upholding today's highest governance standards. Progression can be painful, we've seen that in changes within HP. But it's necessary and healthy."

Yet the firestorm that erupted over her investigation turned out to be anything but healthy. A main purpose of a nonexecutive chairman was to handle board-level affairs, so the chief executive could focus on running the company. The leak investigation, however, overshadowed everything else happening at HP. The company had shown substantial progress since Hurd's arrival—in part because the strategy Fiorina put in place was starting to pay off, and in part because of Hurd's careful attention to costs and operations. But the scandal over boardroom leaks started to pull down the stock price once again, and cast a cloud over Hurd.

Faced with a mess, the board convinced Dunn to resign the following January as chairman, but remain on the board as a director. That proved too timid a response to the swelling leak scandal, however, and a few days later, Dunn resigned entirely. Mark Hurd was given the title of chairman as well as CEO, ending HP's experiment with a new governance structure.

On September 28, 2006, Republican and Democratic members of the House Energy and Commerce Committee met to investigate the Hewlett-Packard affair. The meeting was reminiscent of the Watergate scandals, with Ann Baskins, Ron DeLia, and others who had been directly involved in the investigation invoking the Fifth Amendment of the Constitution and refusing to testify.

Pattie Dunn, who was now suffering from ovarian cancer and had recently had an operation on her liver, declined to take the Fifth. Instead, she sat for hours, as members of Congress heaped scorn upon her.

"This was a plumber's operation that would make Richard Nixon blush were he still alive," said Michigan Democrat John Dingell, who as the longest-sitting member of the House had served during the Watergate scandal. "Calling them the Keystone Cops is an insult to the original Keystone Cops."

"This is not about law, it's about ethics . . . and, I think morality," said Republican Greg Walden of Oregon. "A dark chapter in corporate governance," agreed Democrat Diana DeGette of Colorado.

"Was there no one in this group of very smart people," asked the committee's chairman, Republican Ed Whitfield, "who had the good sense to say 'STOP'?"

On October 3—a week after she testified before Congress, a day before she was charged by California attorney general Bill Lockyer, and just a few days before beginning a new round of chemotherapy for ovarian cancer—Pattie Dunn sat down with my *Wall Street Journal* colleague George Anders and me for dinner at a restaurant at the top of the Bank of America building, overlooking the Golden Gate Bridge.

She continued to refuse to take any personal responsibility for what had happened. "Am I sorry? Do I regret it? Yes," she said. "Am I responsible? No. I'm not management. I have to rely on the usual reliances. If directors think they have to do the role of management, every director of a public company is going to have to resign tomorrow."

I asked her to explain how she viewed what had happened to her during her tumultuous 20 months as nonexecutive chairman of Hewlett-Packard.

"I think I've been at the nexus of a conflict between the old and new ways of governance," she said. "And I made a very rich and powerful enemy without meaning to. He was in a position to finance an extremely effective and elaborate campaign to get me off the board. It went beyond what even he ever expected."

4

Like Pattie Dunn, Frank Zarb never imagined becoming chairman of AIG. The directors all thought that title would belong to Hank Greenberg in his retirement. Yet like Dunn, once the job landed in his lap, he saw it as an opportunity for a complete remake of the company's power structure.

Under Greenberg, the giant insurer had been the epitome of the 20th-century corporation, the legacy of Alfred Sloan and Harold Geneen, with one man absolutely in charge and very few checks on that man's power.

Under Zarb's leadership, AIG was transformed into what many reformers see as the model for the 21st-century corporation, with the jobs of chairman and chief executive split, the board empowered, and major institutional shareholders given an active say in the company's affairs.

Serving as midwife for this remarkable makeover was Zarb's old colleague Arthur Levitt, who had chaired the Securities and Exchange Commission under President Clinton and who became one of the most persistent advocates of change after the corporate scandals hit.

The board's first order of business was to settle the company's regulatory issues with the SEC, the U.S. Department of Justice, and Eliot Spitzer's office. It did that in February of 2006, at a cost of $1.6 billion.

With Levitt's help, the company then reached out to the new powers of the corporate world—people like Rich Ferlauto of the

American Federation of State, County and Municipal Employees, as well as the folks at CalPERS, Institutional Shareholder Services, and Glass Lewis. These activists were consulted on new directors to bring onto the board, and even given what they believed to be a veto over board members. The board was reconstituted, with the new independent directors recruited personally by Zarb, not by the CEO, Martin Sullivan. Most notable among the new faces was Robert Willumstad, a man once considered a candidate for the top job at Citigroup, but who had missed the brass ring and left his job as chief operating officer of the financial giant in July 2005.

In addition, the company's bylaws were changed, to ensure that the separation of the chairman and chief executive jobs was not a temporary change, but a permanent one. Never again, the board decided, should one person have the unchecked authority over the sprawling insurance company that Greenberg had.

"Having a quality CEO and a quality nonexecutive chairman in this environment is better than not having it," Zarb told me afterward. "If it's done right, that's the answer."

The board also eliminated its executive committee, which Levitt saw as a symbol of "board cronyism" and had been used by Greenberg to assure the most important decisions were made by his most trusted directors. Independent board members were required to meet in executive session, without Sullivan or other managers present, at every board meeting.

In a sharp change from AIG's past practice, board members were prohibited from soliciting charitable contributions from the company. "Philanthropic contributions," Levitt told me afterward, "are an item of seduction for boards that is far greater than almost any perquisite." (Ellen Futter, who as president of the American Museum of Natural History had been one of the great beneficiaries of the company's charitable largess, was allowed to stay on the board, but was told the contributions would end. An exception was made to allow for continued gifts to the Asia Society, even though former UN ambassador Richard Holbrooke, another board member, was chairman of that group's board of trustees.)

The board also created a new panel on public policies, headed by Ambassador Holbrooke, to look into the business implications of issues like global warming. In some ways, this was the most striking change undertaken under Zarb, because it seemed to take the AIG board into issues that reached well beyond its fundamental job of assuring shareholders a fair return. Liberal-leaning shareholder activists at places like CalPERS and AFSCME, and even shareholder advisory services like Institutional Shareholder Services and Glass Lewis, had often been accused by corporate leaders of having a liberal agenda that went well beyond providing better returns. The creation of a board-level committee, headed by a prominent Democrat, to look into global warming, a favorite issue of the Left, certainly seemed to reinforce that charge. The activists countered that any insurance company that didn't seriously explore the ramifications of climate change was endangering its shareholders, since the result could be huge and unexpected insurance claims.

Just how much AIG changed under Zarb became evident at the AIG shareholders meeting in May of 2006. A year earlier, Ferlauto had sued the company in an effort to replace some members of its board. This time, he attended the annual meeting, and in a rare gesture, stood up to publicly praise the board:

I think you've done a very credible job in rebuilding a board with strong, independent, highly qualified candidates so that we have now, I believe, a board that's in place that can help AIG move ahead as it faces future chanlleges. . . .

I think there is an opportunity to prove that corporate

governance really does work. That the relationship between the board, a strong management team and shareholders as equal partners [who] are ready, willing and [able, is] in fact in the future the only way that we can draw a strong and viable business that will create shareholder value for the long term.

He particularly commended the company for becoming "the first insurance company that has put together a global climate risk program that I think serves as a model for others."

While AIG was diving headlong into the new world of corporate power, Hank Greenberg stubbornly and loudly defended the old.

Unlike the company, he refused to settle the charges against him. He continued to fight Spitzer, and even sued the company he had built. He continued to control some 16 percent of the shares of AIG, through his personal holdings and through his continued control of Starr International, which had been created as a vehicle for rewarding top executives and controlled a huge chunk of AIG stock. Yet he used his new perch as the head of a closely related C. V. Starr to go into business in direct competition with AIG, particularly in China.

Greenberg, never fond of taking direction, also refused the advice of lawyers who told him to keep quiet while the investigation proceeded. Instead, he took every opportunity to fire away at Zarb, at regulators and prosecutors, and at the new business climate.

"I could not have built AIG in the current environment," he said in a luncheon speech at New York Law School in April of 2006. Excessive regulation, overzealous prosecutors, new corporate governance rules—all of them worked together, he argued, to prevent the kind of successful company building that he did for nearly four decades.

In an interview with Kimberley Strassel of the *Journal*'s editorial page, he expanded on the theme. After Enron, he said,

> *the regulators became far more aggressive, threatening boards of directors with all kinds of dire things if they didn't do certain things. What happens? The board simply takes over. And when that happens you don't have a company that is thinking about innovation or risk-taking. . . . And once you stop thinking about risk and thinking only about compliance, you are no longer going to be a growth company.*

Greenberg expressed many of the same themes in a conversation with me at about the same time. "Boards can't run companies," he insisted. The idea of having a separate chief executive and chairman appalled him, as did boards meeting in executive session, without management present. It creates an unhealthy "us-versus-them" mentality, he argued. Even the notion of boards filled with independent directors, instead of managers and former managers of the company, was, in his view, a mistake—although a reality he had bowed to years earlier. "Outside boards don't know as much about the company" as insiders, he argued.

He was particularly contemptuous of the idea that his former company had negotiated changes in its structure with the likes of CalPERS and AFSCME. "You can't try to appease every group out there or you'll ruin your own franchise."

His bottom line: "I think shareholders do better when you have somebody running a company that's running it."

Given all the new pressures on public companies, private, he argued, was the way to go. Asked by Reuters if he would ever consider taking closely held Starr International and C. V. Starr public, Greenberg responded: "Not in my lifetime.

"The public arena has become very difficult for everyone. Why is private equity growing so rapidly? Why did 24 of the 25 largest initial public offerings [in 2005] go to London and Hong Kong?"

He saw his personal problems as emblematic of a broader decline of U.S. competitiveness. "There was a time when we were the only engine of growth," he said. "Now, if I were starting over I'd probably move to China or India."

CHAPTER FOUR

THE NEW POWER ELITE

1

In late July of 2005—barely a month before he died—I sat down with Lewis Platt at a coffee shop in Menlo Park, California. As former CEO of Hewlett-Packard, and as nonexecutive chairman of the board of Boeing, Platt had held a front-row seat for the changes that were roiling corporate America.

Platt was born in New York, but had made his career at HP, spending 33 years there before leaving the top job in 1999. He became chairman of Boeing in December 2003, after Boeing chairman Phil Condit was forced to resign. His record as a CEO was mixed, but his reputation as a man of decency and integrity was widely recognized.

We talked for three hours, mostly about what happened to Harry Stonecipher at Boeing, and some about what happened to Carly Fiorina at Hewlett-Packard.

By that time, Platt had successfully replaced Stonecipher with James McNerney, the former GE executive who sat on the Boeing board with him and had been CEO of the 3M Corporation. McNerney was fairly new at 3M and reluctant to leave. But he was the Boeing board's runaway favorite, and popular with Boeing executives as well. Convincing him hadn't been easy, but with the help of Tom Neff, the chairman of U.S. operations for Spencer Stuart, the board succeeded. One board member gently taunted McNerney, "Do you want to spend your life selling Post-it notes? Or airplanes?" Eventually, McNerney came around.

The Stonecipher affair, Platt said, did show something had

changed in the corporate world. He rejected the idea that boards in the past had been patsies for management. "Many boards, if not most, have always taken their jobs seriously."

But what was new, he said, was that the "patience for poor performance, for failure to change, for failure to act on suggestions of board members, has fallen." And the clear indication of that was the fact that the "tenure of CEOs is plummeting."

He denied that board members, in the new world, are "scared." But he acknowledged that "litigation, new rules and regulations have put board members more on guard. Now, even the courts may hold you liable." And he said shareholders—"particularly large institutional shareholders—are not that patient. Their demands are more explicit."

Platt also highlighted another change in the new world of corporate power. Information traveled much more freely. While the letter that brought down Harry Stonecipher was sent by old-fashioned "snail" mail, Platt said, employees now "didn't hestitate to send e-mail" to the chairman of the board. "It's an informal way of communicating. For an employee to send me an e-mail seems much less threatening than calling me."

In the days of Harold Geneen, CEOs used their control over the information that went to the board as a way of controlling the board. In the new world, information hierarchies were gone. The boards at Hewlett-Packard and at Boeing weren't reliant on the CEO to know what was going on at the company, and as a result, the CEO no longer had the same power over the board that Geneen had had.

I asked Platt if the shift in corporate power that had brought down Fiorina and Greenberg and Stonecipher and Phil Condit before him was just a temporary phenomenum—a short-term reaction to the scandals at Enron and WorldCom.

His response: "Not likely."

Platt had seen, and indeed had been a part of, the shift in power from the chief executive's office to the corporate boardroom. At HP, AIG, Boeing and countless other companies, directors were acting with new energy, dismissing top executives, and creating new structures for running the company. Boosted by the authority granted them in the Sarbanes-Oxley law and in new stock exchange listing requirements, and goaded by the threat of lawsuits, they had been transformed from rubber stamps to independent forces.

Yet there was clearly more going on here than a simple shift of power from CEOs to boards of directors. Boards, in many cases, were reacting to strong forces outside the boardroom. In each case examined in this book, the board felt intense pressure from others. The Hewlett-Packard board was hearing from investors, analysts and employees who were unhappy with Fiorina's leadership—and later from politicians, journalists and a host of others who were unhappy with Dunn's investigation. The AIG directors had the hot breath of Eliot Spitzer burning down their backs—as well as that of an accountant who refused to sign the company's books. The Boeing directors were acutely aware of their critics in Congress, led by Senator John McCain, who were threatening to shut down the company's government business over ethical breaches.

In many of the CEO firings, the boards of directors resisted action as long as they could. Morgan Stanley's board, for instance, stayed loyal to CEO Phil Purcell until it became clear that the forces bearing down on them—hedge funds, pension funds, former executives, current executives threatening to leave their jobs—could no longer be resisted. Bristol-Myers Squibb's board likewise showed remarkable loyalty to troubled CEO Peter Dolan, and only dismissed him after a court-appointed monitor said bluntly that he had to go.

In the new corporate world, it seemed, power had been widely dispersed. As CEO authority declined in the early 2000s, a host of new players rushed in, all eager to have their say in the running of large public companies. Ambitious regulators and attorneys general, opportunistic hedge funds, activist pensions funds, entrepreneurial nongovernmental organizations, even employees with a simple e-mail connection to the board, all saw a chance to increase their influence. With the popularity of corporate America at record lows, and the authority of CEOs under challenge, "corporate governance" became a power game that all sorts of ambitious people could play.

Many of these new players had begun their careers in politics, using the traditional tools of democracy as a means to achieve their ends. But the conservative takeover of government in the 1980s and 1990s, and the increasing stalemate that characterized Washington, had led them to seek other routes to power. The corporation, no longer the exclusive preserve of high-profile CEOs, turned out to be fertile ground for their efforts.

This chapter is an introduction to some of those new power players.

2 ||||||||||||||||||||||||||||||||||

Pension Funds

Richard Ferlauto is not the sort of guy you would expect to find hanging around a corporate boardroom.

A New Jersey native, he has spent most of his life as an advocate for liberal causes. He started working as an organizer of low-income housing residents in Connecticut, advised New Jersey Senate Democrats on housing issues, started an affordable housing center at Rutgers University, and worked as a policy director for the liberal-leaning Center for Policy Alternatives, based in Washington. Today, he works for the American Federation of State, County and Municipal Employees, one of the most powerful labor unions in the country.

In the new order, Ferlauto may be one of the most important people in corporate America. When John Mack replaced Phil Purcell as head of Morgan Stanley, one of the first calls he made was to Ferlauto. When Pattie Dunn became chairman of Hewlett-Packard, she sought a meeting with Ferlauto as well. AIG chairman Frank Zarb boasted of the fact that Ferlauto stood up at his annual meeting and praised the company's governance changes in 2006. Home Depot chief executive Robert Nardelli complained that Ferlauto orchestrated the sabotage of his annual meeting that same year.

Ferlauto's first taste of boardroom action came in 1983, when he helped organize an historic event in which 100 farmworkers walked 600 miles from Toledo, Ohio, to the headquarters of the Campbell's Soup Company in Camden, New Jersey, to attend the company's annual meeting.

The farmworkers were concerned that Campbell's subcontractors were paying low wages and poor benefits to tomato pickers, and stood up to make their case at the meeting. In an unusual scene, corporate gadfly Evelyn Y. Davis criticized the farmworkers, saying they had too many children, and even suggested they should be sterilized. In response, the chairman of the company, John Dorrance Jr., a descendant of one of the company's early founders, jumped in to defend the farmworkers. He promised to work with them, and a few years later the company signed agreements covering the wages and working conditions for the workers.

For Ferlauto, the meeting was a clear demonstration of how

pressure on corporations could lead to progressive results. The meeting was also where he met his wife, who had helped to organize the farmworkers.

Ferlauto's more serious boardroom indoctrination began in 1996, when he was hired to help the AFL-CIO's Office of Investment Policy. Union boss John Sweeney had recognized that the big pools of pension money held by the labor unions and by the public worker pension funds could be a powerful tool. He hired Ferlauto to figure out how to wield it.

Later, Ferlauto joined Institutional Shareholder Services, but continued working with union pension funds and public pension funds, advising them on how to vote their corporate proxies. He grew disillusioned with ISS because he felt it wasn't being aggressive enough in opposing some mergers—such as Hewlett-Packard's plan to merge with Compaq—and decided to return to the union world, joining AFSCME as its director of pension policy.

AFSCME itself has a relatively modest pension plan—totaling about $800 million. But AFSCME's members are big participants in public employee pension plans around the country, which have a combined total of about $1 trillion in assets. As Ferlauto figures it, AFSCME members indirectly own in the neighborhood of 4 percent of the shares of every large public company in the country—enough to give them clout. His job was to try to organize that shareholder clout. With the giant mutual funds siding with management in most corporate proxy fights, there was little chance for Ferlauto and his allies to win majority votes. They learned, however, that a sizable minority was enough to embarrass many companies and achieve their ends.

In an early "victory," for instance, Ferlauto won the support of 28 percent of Lockheed Martin's shareholders in an effort to kick Frank Savage, who had been a director of Enron, off the defense contractor's board. The effort failed—Savage remained on Lockheed Martin's board—but the vote was enough to embarrass the company, and encourage Ferlauto. A bigger victory came in 2004, when Ferlauto was part of the coalition working to topple Disney chief executive Michael Eisner, which won the support of 43 percent of votes cast by shareholders. Eisner subsequently resigned.

After Disney, Ferlauto found that the corporate world's approach to him changed dramatically. Companies realized they needed to listen to Ferlauto, and possibly even respond to him.

"When I started this 10 years ago," he told me, "we were essentially talking to brick walls. But we have evolved to a point that [companies] have to understand that there has to be some sort of shareholder engagement."

Increasingly, companies started working with Ferlauto in order to avoid embarrassing proxy votes. Insurance broker Marsh & McLennan, for instance, saw Ferlauto and company coming at it with a proxy proposal that would enable large shareholders to nominate directors. In order to head off the threat, the company added attorney Zachary Carter—a candidate favored by AFSCME—to its slate of nominees.

Ferlauto acknowledged his group is opportunistic, looking for companies and issues that grab the public's attention. In 2006, the group pushed a number of proxy proposals that would require companies to give shareholders a nonbinding "advisory" vote on the compensation of executives. While none of those won a majority, several got more than 40 percent of the vote, showing once again the power of the issue.

AFSCME has also spearheaded proxy measures designed to force companies to adopt bylaw changes that would allow major shareholders to put director nominees on the corporate proxy ballot. Under existing rules, any effort to win director seats requires shareholders to launch a complicated and expensive proxy challenge, in which they have to send out their own ballots to shareholders. Some hedge funds are willing to try that tactic, but most pension funds are unwilling to spend the money.

The SEC considered changes in 2005 that would make it easier for large shareholders to nominate directors, but they were scuttled after an intense campaign from big business. So Ferlauto took another route, offering proxy measures that would change a company's bylaws to allow for nomination of directors.

When the Securities and Exchange Commission ruled that companies could exclude the controversial AFSCME measure from their proxies, the union went to court—eventually winning a favorable ruling from the U.S. Court of Appeals of the Second Circuit. Ferlauto argued that the court's ruling would become the most important change in shareholder rights in decades, allowing groups like his to start nominating directors of their own.

Business groups argue that unions like AFSCME have a hidden agenda of promoting union workforces. Ferlauto counters that his group focuses on "process changes" with the intention of increasing returns to shareholders. His job, he says, is to ensure union workers get their pensions, not to fight union battles in the boardroom.

While he acknowledges sweeping changes in recent years, Ferlauto believes boards of directors still aren't stepping up to the plate on tough issues like executive pay. Nor is he impressed by the fact that so many CEOs have been fired.

"We are not looking necessarily for CEO firings," he says. "We are looking for CEOs that can do the job for shareholders. And we are looking for boards that can create stability for shareholders for the long term."

Shareholder Advisory Services

Patrick McGurn is an unassuming man—serious, low-key, slightly wonkish. Yet in the new world of corporate power, he's a heavyweight.

McGurn is executive vice president of Institutional Shareholders Services, and as such makes recommendations to the firm's 1,700 clients—largely institutional investors—on how to vote their corporate proxies. He downplays the importance of that role—dismissing the "mythology that our clients follow our recommendations in lock step." But anyone in the corporate world who has been on the wrong side of an ISS recommendation knows just how important the group can be. An ISS recommendation can mean the end of a career for a director or CEO.

Unlike Rich Ferlauto, McGurn, age 46, came to corporate activism from the conservative end of the political spectrum. He began his career in the 1980s working for Nevada senator Paul Laxalt— known in Washington as Ronald Reagan's best friend—while earning a law degree at Georgetown University in the evenings. When Laxalt left to run the Republican National Committee, McGurn went with him; and when Laxalt briefly flirted with a presidential run himself, McGurn was there.

His emergence as corporate activist came in 1986, when another ex–Laxalt aide, Ralph Whitworth, persuaded Texas oilman T. Boone Pickens to start a group called United Shareholders Association, or USA. The group was set up in reaction to the policies companies were adopting to fight off raiders and hostile takeovers— policies like greenmail, or dual classes of stock. Those tactics, while successful in fending off attackers, often led to clearly outrageous violations of the rights of other shareholders, who didn't get the benefit of greenmail payments or the boost in stock price that might have come from a takeover bid. McGurn helped Whitworth set up the organization. "Shareholders were being abused," McGurn says. "There was a need for investors to step up to the plate."

Soon after, he joined the Investor Responsibility Research Center, which had been founded in 1972 to pressure companies on social issues, like the Vietnam War and apartheid in South Africa, but in the 1980s turned to shareholder rights. Like others in the corporate activist movement, IRRC reflected the odd marriage between those who wanted to use the corporation for social purposes and those who wanted to make capitalism work for the people who provided capital. "There has always been a tension in this business," says McGurn, "between the radical anticorporate crowd and the people who love markets and capitalism. It leads to a lot of infighting."

McGurn left briefly in 1989 to work for a corporate law practice in the Virgin Islands, where many companies had located foreign sales corporations for tax reasons. He arrived on St. Thomas barely a week before Hurricane Hugo hit, leaving him without power for his first three months on the island. After a few years in a staid corporate law practice, however, he was eager to return to Washington, and came back to the IRRC.

At the time, the IRRC was the preeminent organization for researching corporate practices. Bob Monks, who had started ISS in the mid-1980s, suggested that the two organizations combine, with IRRC providing the research and ISS providing the advice. But the board of IRRC decided to stick with research only, and in 1996 McGurn left to join ISS.

His 10 years at the shareholder advisory service have encompassed a period of remarkable growth, as more and more institutional investors have come to realize—prodded in part by government regulators—that they have a fiduciary responsibility to their investors to take an active role in corporate proxy votes.

Institutional investors can use the firm's services in several ways. They can simply take ISS research, without the recommendations, and use it to make their own decisions on how to vote their proxies. They can take ISS's "stock" recommendations, which are the ones that are frequently reported in the press. Or they can get custom recommendations, based on criteria they provide ISS. The firm, for instance, makes separate sets of recommendations for union-based funds, public pension funds, and for investors who are particularly concerned about social issues. In addition, McGurn says, ISS administers as many as 300 customized proxy voting policies.

From where he sits, McGurn sees a dramatic change in the way corporations are run in his ten years on the job. "The paradigm has shifted so far, it's almost unrecognizable," he says.

In the wake of Enron and WorldCom, large mutual funds, which had resisted efforts to get involved in corporate governance, started dipping their toes in the water. New regulations required them to publish their proxy votes, and in response, more of them signed up with ISS and even occasionally started to back activist positions.

As a result of this and other post-Enron changes, McGurn says, ISS has seen "explosive growth for us as an organization. . . . The time and attention our clients pay to these things has grown exponentially."

Many initiatives that ISS backs, which received only minimal support in the 1990s, now regularly receive the support of a majority of shareholders. Votes against antitakeover "poison pills," for instance, often get a majority, and 119 companies recently surveyed by ISS have eliminated poison pills in the last five years. Measures to stop the staggered election of directors, another popular defense against takeovers, also win a majority of votes, on average. As a result, poison pills and staggered director elections now seem clearly on the decline as takeover defenses.

Moreover, ISS and other proxy recommendation services, like Glass Lewis and Proxy Governance Inc., have helped to make boards of directors much more independent of their CEOs. McGurn says that in 2002, ISS recommended votes withheld for reelection of certain directors at some 52 percent of the companies it looked at, in large part because boards or audit committees or nominating committees or overall boards weren't sufficiently independent. By 2006, that was down to 26 percent of companies, even though the ISS standards had, if anything, toughened up in the meantime.

Most important, McGurn says, corporations now regularly sit down with large investors and discuss changes in their corporate governance. Instead of putting up a stone wall, corporations have started talking to the activists, and listening as well.

McGurn says what's happened in the last five years is that "the nexus of power has moved from the corner office to the boardroom." That's a huge change.

But for McGurn and other activists, there's a second step still to be taken. "How do we now get board members to be more accountable to shareholders?" he says. "Is the board a star chamber, only accountable to itself, or is it accountable to shareholders?"

To further that "accountability," ISS and others have been successfully pushing to get companies to adopt majority voting for directors. Under current corporate rules, directors get elected with no more than one vote, provided there are no candidates running against them. Efforts to "withhold" votes from a director serve to make a symbolic protest, but they usually don't keep a director from being elected. The provisions backed by ISS and others would require a director to win a majority of the votes cast, in order to win election. That will increase the power of activists to knock off directors they don't like.

The next step, backed by McGurn and others, is for the activists to get "proxy access"—the ability to put their own director names on the company's proxy ballot. That campaign may take years to play out, but if it's successful, corporate boards could be transformed from clubby groups of people who select their own members to diverse groups representing the interests of an assortment of shareholders.

Will any of his guarantee better performance for shareholders? Or will more diverse routes to the boardroom lead to more conflicts of the HP variety?

"There is no guaranteed formula that says if you put this in place, you'll have good performance," says McGurn. But he does say that in the last few years, some research has suggested good governance practices are correlated with good performance.

The one thing he believes is absolutely clear is this: If a company has poor governance structures, "it will eventually catch up with you."

Social Activists

"Sister Pat" sits in an office on the edge of Harlem with a stunning view of the Manhattan skyline and a long personal perspective on the shareholder movement.

The mild-mannered, 60-year-old nun is a member of the Sisters of Mercy, and in 1975 she was asked by the president of the Westchester Sisters of Mercy to represent the group at a new organization called the Interfaith Council on Corporate Responsibility. The group was attempting to organize churches and other faith-based organizations to put pressure on corporations to adopt responsible policies, particularly with regard to South Africa.

With an undergraduate degree in government and history, Pat Wolf had no interest in working with corporations. "I said, 'I don't really want to do that.' And she said, 'Patricia, did you hear me? I want you to do this.'"

As executive director of the tristate coalition for responsible investing, she witnessed firsthand some of the early—and not terribly successful—efforts to get corporations to hew to the agendas of outside groups. Then in 1985, she was asked to take on another assignment, and left the "responsible investing" movement behind—until March of 2001, when she was asked to submit an application to become executive director of ICCR. She did, and got the job.

Shortly after that, the scandals of Enron, WorldCom, Adelphia and others grabbed national attention. Under attack, corporations began to realize they couldn't afford to simply ignore outside groups—particularly when those groups represented shareholders.

"One of the most striking differences" between her time pushing shareholder activism in the 1970s and 1980s and her tenure at the top of ICCR in recent years "is the level of seriousness with which corporate leaders now take corporate social responsibility."

In the 1970s, she said, when her group would file a proxy proposal for the annual meeting, they'd usually meet with a corporate lawyer and a public relations representative, who would ask that the resolution be redrawn. Today, the group finds top-level executives are ready to engage. As we sat in her office in July of 2006, she told me that in the past year, the group had held meetings with the chief executives of Merck, Schering-Plough, Johnson & Johnson and Coke. "That would have been unheard of in the 1970s," she said.

ICCR has also met with a variety of independent directors of corporations in the past year.

The group has a variety of issues on its agenda—HIV/AIDS treatment for Africans, human rights violations in the third world, sweat shops, global warming. It engages the companies as shareholders. The religious groups that belong to the coalition have combined shareholdings of about $110 billion.

The group often begins by offering shareholder resolutions. "If the company stonewalls, we will insist it stay on the ballot, and we go to the annual meeting and speak." The group offered 137 such shareholder resolutions in 2006.

But increasingly, to avoid these resolutions, companies are choosing to sit down and negotiate with ICCR. As a result, says Sister Pat, "50 percent of our time is now spent in direct engagement with corporate leaders."

An example of the pattern of engagement in recent years is the group's interaction with PepsiCo. Having worked with Coca-Cola on a plan for treating workers in Africa with AIDS, the group in 2002 sponsored a shareholder resolution asking Pepsi to study its policies to help AIDS. The company initially opposed the resolution, and argued that unlike Coca-Cola, Pepsi's presence in Africa was minimal.

Mark Regier, who coordinates socially responsible investing for MMA Financial Services, a Mennonite investing firm, took the lead for ICCR in its negotiation with Pepsi. He said the group was largely ignored the first and second years it offered the resolution. But at the annual meeting the third year, CEO Steven Reinemund pledged to address the issue. A representative of ICCR asked the company to visit its operations in South Africa, and members of PepsiCo's human resources department went along.

PepsiCo eventually developed a policy for dealing with the global AIDS epidemic. When ICCR objected that it was too tame—it

mostly involved posters and free condoms—the company went back
to the drawing board and came up with a more detailed policy.

"It was a sign of real respect," says Regier. "I credit Mr. Reinemund with that."

5 ||||||||||||||||||||||||||||||||

Hedge Funds

For CEOs under attack, Martin Lipton has long been the lawyer of
choice. During the era of raiders and hostile takeovers, he helped
corporate leaders build the ramparts that kept them safe.

It was Lipton who, in 1982, invented the "poison pill"—a mechanism designed to thwart takeovers by giving other shareholders the
rights to acquire more stock if one tried to buy a controlling share.
Poison pills were used frequently to fend off raiders like Carl Icahn.
But they are the bane of shareholder activists, because they deny
shareholders the opportunity to benefit from the higher stock prices
that result from takeover battles. Remarkably, the courts in Delaware—where most companies are registered—ruled Lipton's poison
pills to be legal.

So the corporate world took note in December of 2005, when
Lipton's annual briefing memo warned there was a new wolf howl-
ing at the corporate door. The number one issue for his clients, he
wrote, was "anticipating attacks by activist hedge funds seeking
strategy changes by the company to boost the price of the stock."

As the stock market swooned in 2000 and 2001, hedge funds soared. They were large pools of private money designed to help investors make money at a time when the overall stock market returns were listless. They required a large minimum investment—often as much as $1 million—and had a relatively small number of investors—fewer than 500. As a result, they were able to escape the regulations imposed on mutual funds, which were designed to protect smaller investors.

Hedge funds pursued a wide array of investment strategies—some sold stocks short in anticipation of a drop, others tried to anticipate events that would move markets, and still others put together complicated arrays of exotic investment instruments designed to benefit not from market trends, but from the volatility of markets. They had little in common except this: all of them promised their investors (but didn't always achieve) high rates of return, and all of them reaped huge fees for their managers—who took anywhere from 20 percent to 50 percent of the money they earned for their investors. As the hedge fund business grew, top hedge fund managers became the new financial elite, earning tens of millions, hundreds of millions, or in a few cases, even a billion dollars a year.

By 2005, hedge funds were said to control more than $1 trillion a year in assets. Their influence in financial markets was magnified many times over for two reasons: (1) they operated with heavy borrowing, or leverage, allowing them to turn their $1 trillion into four or five times that much investment, and (2) they were willing to move quickly—much more quickly than traditional investors.

Just one hedge fund alone—Steven Cohen's SAC Capital—was said to account for 2 percent of the stock market's trading volume on a normal day, and much more on an active day. Cohen controlled $10 billion in funds. His oldest and most successful charged a 3 percent fee and kept 50 percent of the profits, but still delighted investors with returns exceeding 40 percent a year. Like many hedge fund managers, Cohen lived in leafy Greenwich, Connecticut. His home was a sprawling estate that included a basketball court, an indoor pool, a skating rink, two holes of golf and a 20-seat movie theater. It was decorated with an art collection valued at nearly $1 billion, including paintings by Jackson Pollock, Vincent van Gogh, Gauguin, Andy Warhol and Roy Lichtenstein.

As the control of corporate leaders weakened, some hedge funds saw an opportunity. They could move in, buy up shares, and force CEOs to adopt strategies that would boost the share price. A common tactic was to push for share buybacks. With profits strong from 2003 to 2005, many companies were accumulating large piles of cash. While CEOs might prefer to save that cash for future projects, activist funds pushed them to buy back shares of their stock in order to push up the stock price.

In some cases, activist hedge funds got even more venturesome. They would intervene to push managers to sell off parts of their business. Or they might lead the charge against an ineffective CEO.

Hedge funds played a key role in toppling Morgan Stanely chief Phil Purcell. Scott Sipprelle, a former Morgan Stanley executive and chairman of hedge fund firm Copper Arch Capital, started buying up the firm's stock in late 2004. Then he wrote a letter to Purcell, pushing him to sell off the Discover credit card business or the firm's brokerage business. In early March, eight prominent Morgan Stanley alumni publicly called for Purcell's removal, leading more hedge funds, smelling a chance for a quick buck, to buy up the firm's stock. Eventually, big pension funds joined the battle as well. By June 30, 2005, Purcell was gone.

Feeling their increased power, hedge funds started to get more creative. In September 2005, William Ackman of Pershing Square Capital Management LP bought options entitling him to a 4.9 percent stake in McDonald's. After stumbling briefly at the beginning of the decade, McDonald's had recovered nicely, and ranked near the top of Dow Jones Industrial Average companies in providing a return to shareholders. But Ackman thought the company wasn't doing enough. So he drew up a detailed plan for restructuring the company, calling for spinning off some of its stores, borrowing heavily against its real estate holdings, and buying back shares to boost the stock price.

Ackman offered an extraordinary detailed proposal—the sort that an investment bank might make if it were hired by the company. In order to get other investors to follow his lead, he rented a hotel room near Times Square in New York City, and gave a PowerPoint presentation in person and via Web conference to several hundred people. He argued that McDonald's should spin off all 8,000 of its company-owned stores, and use the money it raised to buy back shares. Never before in anyone's memory had an outside investor made such a detailed public proposal for changing a company's strategy.

A few days later, Ackman got at least a part of what he wanted. The company said it would convert at least 1,500 of the stores it owned to franchises, and would buy back $1 billion in shares. It was only a fraction of the Ackman plan, but the hedge fund investor claimed victory, declaring, "I got what I wanted." McDonald's chief financial officer, Matthew Paull, warned that the Ackman attack showed a new era had begun, in which investors could second-guess the strategy of corporate managers. "The message has been sent," he said. "No company is safe."

In 2006, Ackman participated in another hedge fund attack, this one led by longtime investor Nelson Peltz against the H. J. Heinz Company. The company's chief executive, William Johnson, fought back, resulting in one of the nastiest name-calling battles in modern corporate history, all over how to sell ketchup.

The quality of the debate was captured in an exchange that, according to Peltz, took place in March 2006 at a dinner the two men had at a Morton's restaurant in Florida. Peltz says he told Johnson the company needed to spend more money marketing ketchup. Johnson responded that he already had 70 percent of the ketchup market. Peltz then said that only 30 percent of people use ketchup on their french fries, "so you only have 70 percent of 30 percent. You've got to get 70 percent of 90 percent."

Later, the pesky investor suggested that Johnson erred by not cosponsoring the World Championship Hot Dog Eating Contest—won that year by Takeru Kobayashi, who downed just short of 54 hot dogs, without ketchup, in 12 minutes.

Peltz and his group, which owned just 5.5 percent of the company's shares, managed to get a slate of five directors on the company's ballot in August. Two of them—Peltz included—were elected. Once again, hedge funds had shown themselves to be powerful players in the running of large corporations.

The boldest hedge fund attack of 2006 came courtesy of a name from the past, onetime raider Carl Icahn. Older but no less feisty, Icahn started buying up stock in the media giant Time Warner, hoping other hedge funds would follow his lead and buy shares. A few did—most notably Steven Cohen of SAC Capital. Icahn's argument: Time Warner had become an unwieldy behemoth, and needed to sell off some of its businesses, then use the proceeds to buy back shares.

Icahn's most surprising gambit was to hire investment banker Bruce Wasserstein of Lazard Ltd. to do a detailed study of the potential for breaking up the $75 billion company. Wasserstein's involvement stunned many in corporate America. Investment banks never did such detailed work for outside investors, in part because they risked angering the big companies that provided the bulk of their business. But the world had changed, and Wasserstein's move was reflecting that change.

In the end, the Icahn effort produced little—in part because other hedge funds chose not to follow the onetime raider's lead. But Time Warner CEO Dick Parsons had to devote many months to fending off the attack. The mere fact that a giant company like Time Warner could be pushed around by hedge funds showed how much the world had changed.

6

Nongovernmental Organizations

In November of 2004, a group of schoolchildren from Fairfield County, Connecticut—a lush suburban region that is home to many of the nation's top CEOs—were led down to the Manhattan head-quarters of the J.P. Morgan Chase Bank. They were carrying their own drawings of rain forests, and letters and posters calling on the bank's chief executive—William Harrison—to "protect the rainforest instead of hurting the earth for oil."

The organization behind this stunt was the Rainforest Action Network, a small group of activists with a radical agenda that's based in San Francisco. RAN has emerged as one of the most effective environmental groups in the country. The reason: It has given up trying to get change from a gridlocked government in Washington, and instead has focused its attention on influencing corporations.

A decade or two ago, that approach would have been a recipe for frustration, as gadflies like James Peck and Saul Alinsky discovered. But in the new corporate climate, RAN found it could get surprising results. Besieged by the anticorporate sentiment that set in after the scandals of 2001 and 2002, and dependent on the goodwill associated with their brand names, many big companies opened up—some would say bowed down—to groups like RAN in ways they never had before.

The group had honed its skills in a long-running campaign against Home Depot, the home improvement store chain, during the 1990s. Its goal was to get Home Depot stores to stop selling old-growth lumber from the rain forests and redwood forests. In 1998, it launched what amounted to a guerrilla campaign against the company, staging demonstrations at stores with protesters chaining themselves to piles of lumber and hijacking the stores' PA systems to denounce selling of rain forest wood.

Celebrities pitched in, with musical groups like the Dave Matthews Band and R.E.M. joining the cause. RAN also took out large advertisements in publications like the *New York Times* and others, denouncing Home Depot.

Finally, the company caved. It agreed to a set of policies to stop sales of old-growth lumber.

"It was huge win for us," says Michael Brune, executive director of RAN, who was brought on to run the Home Depot campaign. "The change was immediate." Once Home Depot had agreed, RAN found it could easily get its competitors, like Lowe's and Wickes to fall in line.

Behind RAN's successes is Brune, the son of a New Jersey politician who was inspired by the example of John F. Kennedy and taught his family that "public service is vital . . . that we have an obligation to make the world a better place."

Brune studied economics at West Chester University in Pennsylvania and gave some thought to going into business, but instead decided to use his awareness of business to help political activists.

He joined the environmental group Greenpeace, where he worked for four years before being recruited to run the Home Depot campaign at the Rainforest Action Network. It was 1998, and he was 27 years old.

After its success with lumber, Brune led the group in its attack on the big banks. It started with Citigroup, sending a letter to chairman Sandy Weill, demanding that the global financial conglomerate stop lending money for logging, mining and oil-drilling projects that destroy rain forests, threaten indigenous people and accelerate global warming. It staged protests at bank branches, and urged customers to cut up their Citi cards.

At first the bank ignored the campaign. But RAN grew more clever in its attacks, repelling down the side of the company's midtown headquarters to unfurl a giant banner that said "Forest Destruction and Global Warming? We're Banking on It!" It ran commercials on cable TV that featured stars like Ed Asner, Susan Sarandon and Darryl Hannah cutting their Citi cards. And it shadowed Weill when he traveled, running full-page advertisements with his picture, labeling him an environmental villain.

These were mostly nuisance tactics that never threatened the bank's core business. But Citi's reputation was already under attack, as a result of its role in the Enron, WorldCom and other scandals. So it finally gave in, working with RAN on a series of lending principles based on "a common understanding of key global sustainable development issues." The guerrillas of RAN became a Citi partner, of sorts, invited into the company's headquarters to meet with top executives, including new chief executive Chuck Prince.

After getting Citi to agree, RAN followed the path it had pioneered in the lumber campaign—start with the industry leader, then move through the rest of the industry. So it launched a campaign against J.P. Morgan Chase. Among other tactics, it put "Wanted" posters up throughout Harrison's leafy Greenwich, Connecticut, neighborhood. J.P. Morgan Chase eventually agreed to a set of lending principles with RAN, as did the rest of the industry.

How important were these agreements? All the banks involved insist they didn't agree to anything that would affect the companies' bottom lines. But some of the developing countries who saw big bank lending dry up as a result might have a different view.

In a meeting in Brune's San Francisco offices, I asked him whether these environmental issues shouldn't really be sorted out by the political process, rather than by companies. He agreed. "Governments were set up to deal with these issues," he said. "And they should. But they are not." As a result, pressuring corporations—which seem more willing to respond to such pressure than they have in the past—"is the best way of affecting change right now. We are using corporations as a way to effect public policy."

There's an irony here. RAN's environmental agenda is well to the left of the average American. When I interviewed Ilyse Hogue, who led the global finance campaign, she confessed she'd be happy if the big banks stopped all lending to oil companies. Indeed, RAN seems pretty nearly opposed to any sort of extractive industry, and not inclined to worry about the costs that might be associated with its proposals. Brune, a picture of reason in his interview with me, denied this. Still, it is clear that one reason he and other environmental groups have so far found little success in public policy debates is because the American public doesn't necessarily agree with them.

So instead, the group has made its mark by pressuring the corporations that, in RAN's own demonology, mark the dangerous right wing of the spectrum. Corporate America has, in a bizarre twist of affairs, become a standard-bearer for the left-wing agenda.

Much of the credit for this goes to Brune and his organization, which has been very strategic in the way it approaches these companies. It looks for companies that have a large brand that needs to be protected. And it seems to look for companies that are vulner-able, as Citigroup was, and as the Ford Motor Company—the target of RAN's more recent campaign—is.

"We train our organizers to think like a CEO," says Brune. The group's real target, he explains, is the oil companies. But they are happy to ignore RAN's guerrilla tactics. So instead, the group has targeted an industry that is responsible for consuming much of that oil, and a company whose CEO pays lip service to environ-mental virtue. "We are trying to drive a wedge between Houston and Detroit."

One of RAN's partners in the latest effort is the Ruckus Society, a group that honed its skills during the antiglobalization protests at the turn of the century. A visit to the Ruckus Society Web site shows that is specialty is training protesters in extreme tactics. At the top of the list: "How to Hang Yourself from an Urban Structure." A caveat: "Only an experienced climber can comprehend and prac-tice this form of direct action," the site warns. "You will get hurt if attempting this without proper training, setting the movement for social justice, environmental security and human rights back in the eyes of the world."

As Brune sees it, these tactics aren't hurting corporations; they are saving them from themselves. In Ford's case, for instance, the group is asking the company to unilaterally raise the fuel efficiency levels of its fleet. "We think this is a way they can resuscitate the company."

He acknowledges the arrogance of that position. "How can some smug, 30-something punks in San Francisco who've never run a company before have the gall to think they have the secret to save this company?" His answer? A smile.

RAN's successes have clearly helped its fund-raising—it has grown from a $2 million-a-year organization a couple of years ago to a $3 million organization in 2006 and a $4 million organization in

2007. Brune is frequently invited to speak to other groups, and help them understand his approach.

The goal of all this is nothing less than a new model for capitalism. "We're not calling for abolition of the corporation," he says. "Capitalism has enabled us to achieve amounts of wealth we would not have dreamed of 100 or 150 years ago. But I'd like to believe we've learned something in the process."

"Are we screwing up the public company?" he asks. "I would say we are saving it. I don't think it's going to be possible for public companies to survive without being good neighbors."

While Michael Brune tries to use corporate power to advance his liberal agenda, Randy Sharp is doing the same for his Christian conservative one.

Sharp is a part of the American Family Association, which has targeted Ford because of its advertisements in gay and lesbian publications and its support for gay and lesbian groups and events. The group argues that Ford is undercutting the family in the process.

In many ways, the AFA campaign has been even more damaging to Ford than RAN's campaign. The group has targeted Ford dealers in the South and Southwest, where Christian conservatives are particularly strong, and called on supporters to boycott Ford cars. Some dealers have told the company that the campaign is costing them sales.

But when Ford tried to sit down and talk with the AFA, it found itself the target of another campaign, led by gay and lesbian employees and other outside groups. As one frustrated Ford executive told me, "This is one we can't win."

Private Equity

When the Business Council held its meeting in Washington in May 2006, it had an unusual new member in its midst: private-equity king Henry Kravis.

Two decades earlier, one of Kravis's deals had been the subject of the book *Barbarians at the Gate*—and Kravis had been the barbarian. He and his colleagues in the private-equity world were outsiders—not part of the club of public company CEOs who controlled the lion's share of the U.S., and the world, economy.

By 2006, however, private equity had gone mainstream. Private-equity funds were raising enormous amounts of money, and snapping up large companies like auto rental company Hertz and hospital company HCA that had once seemed far out of their reach. There was even serious talk about private-equity purchases of automakers General Motors and Ford, and home construction giant Home Depot.

Public company CEOs and their advocates like to point to the explosion in private-equity deals and argue it is proof that the burdens of being a public company have grown too great. Companies go private to avoid the multimillion-dollar accounting costs required by Sarbanes-Oxley, they say, and to avoid the hassles of catering to short-term-minded shareholders, or public pension funds, or all the other groups that are fighting to have a say in running public companies.

As proof, CEOs point to the story of David Calhoun. The head of General Electric's aircraft engine business, Calhoun was widely regarded in 2006 as a top draft choice to lead almost any public company. He was second-in-command at GE—which had a well-deserved reputation as a CEO training school—but had little chance of ever succeeding GE chief executive Jeff Immelt, who had just turned 50. He won raves as a manager from bosses, colleagues and subordinates. Any board of directors in search of a new chief executive would have been happy to have him. But Calhoun pushed aside all such possibilities to take a job running a half-Dutch company, VNU, which was being taken over by a group of private-equity funds.

By most measures, it was a huge step backward. As vice chairman of General Electric, Calhoun ran a $47 billion portfolio of businesses that made big stuff: airplane engines, trains, power turbines, water-treatment plants. In his new job, as chief executive of VNU, he oversees Nielsen television ratings and publications like the *Hollywood Reporter*. Total revenues are just one-tenth those of the businesses he commanded at GE.

Calhoun insisted to me that the money wasn't what motivated him to make the unusual move. But money was clearly significant. Before he left GE, word on the street was that it would take $100 million to pry Calhoun away from his longtime home. Under attack from shareholders and activists, no public company was willing to pay that much. For a private-equity deal the size of VNU, on the other hand, a nine-digit pay package was pretty standard fare. VNU's investors had $4 billion of equity in the deal and hoped to cash out five or so years hence for two and a half to three times that. That would be a gain of $6 billion to $8 billion, and normally management would get 5–7 percent of that, with the CEO taking a third or more of the total.

A key, however, is that unlike many public-company CEOs, Calhoun had to deliver for his investors in order to make that payday.

His private-equity bosses guaranteed him tens of millions of dollars to make up for money he left on the table at GE, but then persuaded him to invest much of that back into VNU—meaning he could end up worse off than before, if the deal collapses. Few publicly traded company CEOs have that kind of skin in the game.

Those who know Calhoun say he was also acutely aware of the growing hassles of running a big publicly traded company in the post-Enron world. Modern CEOs have to kowtow to a long list of folks who want a say in the business. Private-company CEOs, for the most part, only answer to their private-equity investors. Those folks could be every bit as demanding as a Carl Icahn or Eliot Spitzer, but at least they share the same goal—making money—and roughly the same time frame for doing so—three to five years.

In short, private equity offered Calhoun more money, and less hassle. Who could be surprised at his choice?

Also driving the rapid growth in private investing are the decisions by big pension funds to invest ever more in the sector. The early pioneers in this kind of investing, like the Yale Endowment, enjoyed huge returns, and now other pension funds are pouring in to imitate the early investors.

For the reform-minded public pension funds, that creates a huge irony that few are willing to acknowledge. On the one hand, these big pension funds led the push to make public companies more transparent and more responsive to shareholders, and less excessive in their executive pay packages. On the other hand, the same pension funds are fueling a boom in private-equity investments that are creating companies that are far less transparent, far less responsive to any outside interests, and far more generous in their pay packages.

I asked Patricia Macht, assistant executive officer for public affairs at CalPERS, how the giant pension fund justified putting ever-more money into private companies, even as it was putting ever-more demands on public companies. Her answer: "It's not possible for us to revolutionize private equity because everyone wants access to them."

Some observers say private equity has become the new model for corporate ownership in the 21st century. If true, it would reverse the trend toward democratization of wealth that occurred over the previous century. As more companies move to private equity, more wealth is concentrated in the hands of the more fortunate few who can invest in those pools—plus the pension funds now moving this direction.

Such predictions, however, ignored a fundamental reality of the private-equity world. These are relatively short-term investment pools, meant to last only five or 10 years. At the end of the day, investors expected to get their money out of the partnership. And the best way to do that is to sell the company back into the public markets.

For all the buzz private equity is generating, it may be only a temporary respite from the rapid changes facing public companies. Without a strong public market, the private-equity model would cease to exist. Even private-equity companies have to prepare themselves for the inevitable return to the tumultuous public-company world.

CHAPTER FIVE

THE NEW CEO

1 ||||||||||||||||||||||||||||||||

If there is one group of people that understands how profoundly the world of corporate power has changed in the last few years, it is CEOs themselves. I've talked to dozens in the last two years, and each has his or her own story of epiphany. Those who are new to the job—and given the rapid rate of CEO turnover, that's most of them— recognize they have a profoundly different set of responsibilities than their predecessors. The few who have been in the job for five or six years have lived through the revolution.

In 2002, when the corporate scandals of Enron and WorldCom and Tyco were in full flower, I was hosting a nightly television show on CNBC. We would routinely invite CEOs to come on the show to talk about what was happening. And they would routinely turn us down. The business community's early response to the scandals was to argue they were the work of "a few bad apples." Yet no CEO was willing to publicly come to the defense of the barrel. Their lawyers warned them that making such appearances was courting trouble. How confident could they be, after all, that there weren't a few Enron-style problems buried in their own books? Better to keep their heads down and hope the anticorporate mood soon passed.

But it didn't pass. By the time I was invited to meet with members of the Business Council in March of 2006, all of them understood that their world had been transformed. Each of them was struggling to find the right way to respond.

The CEO job, while powerful, can also be a lonely one. Decisions stop at the top, and so does responsibility and blame. The prosecutions of Kenneth Lay and Jeffrey Skilling, former CEOs of Enron; or Bernie Ebbers, former CEO of WorldCom, only served to reinforce the heavy burden that rests upon the CEO's shoulders. Lay died before his sentencing, but Skilling was sentenced to 24 years in prison and Ebbers was sentenced to 25 years—even though the actual fraud at each company was committed by people lower down in the organization.

The effort to redefine the CEO job in the new environment has also been a lonely struggle. There is no template, no right answer to the problem. The only thing that is clear is that in the new environment—with the growing independence of boards, the increased activism of pension funds, the heightened scrutiny of regulators, the new clout of NGOs, the muscular presence of hedge funds and private equity, and most important, the diminished support of the public—the old rules no longer apply. You can't run a big company the way, say, Jack Welch ran General Electric or Sandy Weill ran Citigroup.

GE's Jeffrey Immelt has been one of the leaders in the effort to redefine the CEO. He's reached out to his company's critics, he's imposed measures to limit GE's emissions of the greenhouse gasses that lead to global warming even though the government hasn't mandated such limits, and he's even limited his own pay to appease public complaints.

In a column in late 2005, I wrote that Immelt's actions made him look more like a politician than like the autocratic CEOs of old. That prompted an angry response from Gary Sheffer, the guardian of the Immelt image, who took offense at the comparison because, he thought, it suggested the GE chief executive was more interested in polishing his image than in attending to his company. I would put it a little differently. As I see it, Immelt recognizes that to do his job well, he has to keep the support of a broad group of new constitu-

encies. That requires the skills and efforts and actions of a good
politician.

Other CEOs are responding in similar ways. That doesn't necessarily mean the CEO isn't attending to the operations of the company. But I haven't found a CEO yet who doesn't acknowledge that
the new world forces him or her to spend a larger share of work time
and attention on outreach, and thus a smaller share of time and attention on the company's operations.

Moreover, CEOs now find they are constantly campaigning to
keep their jobs. Consider this fact: A decade ago, two-thirds of all
CEOs stayed in their jobs at least until they reached the early-
retirement age of 62. Today, nearly two-thirds of CEOs don't. Instead, they are subject to constant reevaluation and the possibility
that at any time, they may be dumped. Four times as many of the
world's top CEOs were forced out of their jobs in 2005 as in 1995.
Moreover, CEOs increasingly recognize that the forces behind these
trends show no signs of abating. Boards are rapidly becoming more
independent, as directors who won their jobs in an older, CEO-
centric regime retire. Institutional shareholders are becoming more
aggressive, challenging directors and corporate policies more often,
and winning larger percentages of the shareholder vote. Hedge
funds and private-equity funds are accumulating larger piles of
cash, putting even the largest public companies within their reach.
Corporate-focused nongovernmental organizations are raising more
money and growing stronger, as wealthy people with activist inclina-
tions feed the movement toward social entrepreneurship. Politically
ambitious attorneys general still see attacking corporate crime as a
quick way to make a reputation. Underlying it all, the public contin-
ues to view corporate leaders with deep cynicism and distrust.

No social trend lasts forever, and this one won't, either. But all
indications suggest it is still in its upward arc. CEOs are learning
there's little point in fighting the wave.

2 ||||||||||||||||||||||||||||||||||

Lee Scott isn't fighting the sweeping changes in corporate America. He's adapting.

It's not entirely by choice. The Wal-Mart CEO has found himself the target of a well-organized, well-financed campaign designed to convince people that Wal-Mart is bad. Founded and funded by feuding labor unions, two groups—Wal-Mart Watch and Wake Up Wal-Mart—are spending millions to argue that Wal-Mart lowers wages, destroys communities, discriminates against women and Hispanics, provides inadequate health care coverage, and undermines the environment.

In response to this quasi-political campaign, Scott has had to transform himself into a quasi-politician. It's not a natural job for him. He was the ultimate Wal-Mart insider, a logistics expert who was uncomfortable speaking to large groups, and unwilling, as recently as 2003, to sit for a photograph for *Fortune* magazine.

But in late 2004, he realized all that had to change. With the help of Mack McLarty, an Arkansan and former chief of staff to President Clinton, he began to reach out to key Democratic leaders, members of Congress, leaders of minority groups, environmentalists and even Sister Barbara Aires, a Catholic nun and longtime Wal-Mart critic. He became, not just the company's Chief Executive Officer, but its Chief Reputation Officer—spending as much as half of his time in an effort, not to run Wal-Mart stores, but to convince the world that those stores were a force for good.

Wal-Mart's experience is extreme—no other large company

faces such a focused and prolonged attack on its reputation—but it is not unique. Nor is Lee Scott's transformation. Indeed, Scott is in constant contact with a number of other big-company CEOs—like General Electric's Jeff Immelt and Procter & Gamble's A. G. Lafley—who are likewise struggling to redefine their jobs in a world where companies are often held in low esteem and vulnerable to attack from regulators, attorneys general, shareholder groups, hedge funds, nongovernmental organizations, and a host of other outsiders who want a say in corporate affairs.

For Scott, the transformation is especially profound because of the nature of the company he grew up in. Based in the tiny town of Bentonville, Arkansas, Wal-Mart has remained especially free of the imperial trappings of other global companies. The company's headquarters is a low-lying brick building in the middle of Bentonville, and his office is a modest, street-level room on the first floor, with a small aquarium and window looking out on the parking lot. Founded by the legendary Sam Walton, Wal-Mart was known for its discipline, its single-mindedness, its focus on reducing costs above all else. By squeezing the costs out of logistics and merchandising, and by using its dominant position to force its suppliers to do the same, Wal-Mart has been able to offer a vast array of merchandise at prices lower than can be found anywhere else.

But Lee Scott has abandoned that single-mindedness to pursue his broad-ranging campaign.

I went to visit Scott in February of 2006, a week after a headline had run in the *Financial Times* announcing: "Wal-Mart to Buy Only Sustainable Fish." Something was amiss, I thought. Whole Foods, the high-end retailer, was the one who was supposed to be buying "sustainable" fish. Wal-Mart sold *cheap* fish.

But Scott made no apologies. "I sat down a long time ago," he said, "and asked myself: If you had known the issues we face today, what would you have done differently?" Those questions led Scott to rewrite the company's health care plan, to call for a national minimum wage, and to make a number of other changes designed to reduce criticism.

Then he asked himself, "While you deal with today's issues, what are the issues the next generation will have to deal with?" That's the question that led him to the environment . . . and to sustainable fish.

On the fish front, Scott has in effect handed the quality control for his stores' fish products over to a group of nongovernmental organizations. Fish that's caught in the wild can only be sold at a Wal-Mart store if it's been certified by the Marine Stewardship Council, which works to ensure the oceans aren't overfished. And its farm-raised fish, which comes largely from Chile, will also be certified by two separate NGOs.

"I like the word sustainable," Scott says.

The danger, of course, is that by abandoning Sam Walton's single-mindedness, the company will stop doing the one thing that it has traditionally done really well—cut costs. But Scott insists there are few trade-offs here. "There are fewer compromises than we thought," he says.

He points to a plastic bottle on his desk of a product called "Small and Mighty All." It's a concentrated version of Unilever's best-selling laundry detergent. By taking the water out, Unilever is able to save on packaging costs, and Wal-Mart is able to cut transportation costs—and the associated pollution—in half.

The only drawback is that customers are reluctant to buy the smaller bottle because they think they are getting less. So Scott is giving it a boost by making it his "VPI"—volume producing item—for the year. Wal-Mart has shown in the past that it can use its retailing muscle to get consumers to buy certain products, by placing them more prominently in the store and urging store managers to sell more. By pushing "Small and Mighty All," Scott says, he'll both be helping reduce Wal-Mart's costs and helping the environment.

The same goes for his campaign for sustainable fish. "At this point," he says, "we do not see that as having an impact on our competitiveness. Now, will there be a time that these kinds of decisions will raise costs? I think that is entirely possible, and maybe likely." But if higher costs are necessary to, say, protect the oceans, he's willing to pay them.

"The generation of people I work with—like A. G. Lafley, who has been here in this office in the last two months, or Jeff Immelt, who has been in this office in the last three weeks—feel that there is a business reason to do this." With GE, he says, Wal-Mart is working on new lighting that will both lower the cost of bulbs and save electricity. With Pepsi, he's working on a program to recycle plastic water bottles. All of these efforts are good for business, he insists, as well as good for the environment.

Scott's view flies in the face of traditional business theory, which holds that corporations should really focus on only two things: (1) obeying the laws of the regimes they operate in, and (2) maximizing profits and returns for their shareholders. In this view, tasks like protecting the environment, ensuring adequate health care insurance, and protecting society's poorest are the government's responsibility, not the company's.

"To make this world work, I think those two goals still have to be at the center. But I think with what happens in these jobs today, you cannot accept the easy answers. The world today is more complicated."

Part of the complication comes from the global nature of companies like Wal-Mart. If it chooses to, say, shut down operations in certain countries so it can move them to China, "what are our responsibilities to those countries?" he asks. If Wal-Mart simply ignores those questions, it risks undermining the support for free trade that it needs to sustain its business.

Likewise, in the United States, if Wal-Mart ignores criticisms over its pay and benefit policies, or its hiring policies, it risks fueling a political campaign that has the potential to undercut sales. In that respect, Lee Scott's task is more difficult than that of the politician. A politician only needs the support of a majority of voters to survive. Wal-Mart can't really afford to alienate large minorities without seeing its sales affected as a result. While polls show that most Americans still have positive feelings about Wal-Mart, Scott says, "it would be silly to think there aren't people out there who have heard these negative stories and decided not to buy."

3

A. G. Lafley doesn't talk much about his shareholders. Instead, the chairman and chief executive of Procter & Gamble talks about his "stakeholders."

And just who are those stakeholders? Well, there are its 110,000 employees. There are the managers and employees of the many thousands of companies it sells to, as well as those of its thousands of suppliers. There are the more than two and a half billion consumers in more than 160 countries that have the opportunity to buy P&G products. Then there are the communities that all of these people live in.

Add it all up, and it's pretty hard to find anyone in the world who *isn't* a P&G "stakeholder."

Which is why talking with A. G. Lafley about his responsibilities can be so exhausting. He has so much ground to cover, so many different constituencies to keep in mind, so many competing and compelling ideas to stay on top of. He is clearly a man of great energy and effervescence, excited by this global role he feels has been thrust upon him. We talked for nearly an hour, and then the next day, he sent me an e-mail that covered nine more points he had wanted to cover, and then added three more on top of that.

I noted the fact that, with so many constituents to please, he seemed more like a politician than an old-style CEO. Did that bother him?

He shrugged. "Like it or not, we are in a global economy and a global political world. I've concluded I'm in it anyway, and I might as well deal with it anyway."

Lafley didn't start out with the notion that he was becoming some sort of global ambassador. In fact, when he got the top job in June of 2000, the company had its own problems, and Lafley dedicated himself to addressing them. "My head was down for at least a year or a year and a half," he says.

"Then, when my head came up, all hell was breaking loose." By all hell, he means the scandals at Enron, WorldCom, Adelphia, and a growing suspicion among the public that maybe all big businesses were as corrupt as these. The general reaction among CEOs was to, in Lafley's words, "head to the bunkers."

Lafley, however, was one of the first to recognize that the new environment demanded a new kind of CEO. You couldn't just keep your head down, run a good business, and let the rest of the world take care of itself. Big corporations, at the end of the day, were political institutions. And they were under political attack. To survive and thrive, corporations had to be defended.

That's not always easy. Lafley got a taste of the political complexities when his company agreed to back legislation in its home city of Cincinnati intended to eliminate discrimination against homosexuals. Two religious conservative groups—the American Family Association and Focus on the Family—argued that the ordinance would actually give special privileges to homosexuals, and launched a boycott of P&G products, including Tide laundry detergent and Crest toothpaste. The two groups also complained about the company's advertisements on television shows that featured homosexuals, like *Will and Grace* and *Queer Eye for the Straight Guy.*

P&G officials don't like to talk publicly about the boycott. But privately, they will acknowledge that the Christian conservative groups turned out to be larger, better funded, better organized and more sophisticated than the company had ever imagined. Tim Wildmon, president of the American Family Association, says 360,000 families signed petitions to boycott the P&G products.

Lafley met with representatives of the groups to hear their complaints. And P&G's advertising disappeared from gay magazines and Web sites and gay-oriented television shows. But it didn't change its stance on the boycott.

"We stuck to our guns and principles during that boycott, over an ordinance clearly aimed at gays and lesbians," he insists, "and we won."

Lafley also found himself engaging with People for the Ethical Treatment of Animals, a group upset about the testing of P&G products on animals. When the Procter & Gamble bought Iams, the dog food company, Lafley made sure it had a "state-of-the-art" facility for feeding tests.

"We will never agree that a rat is as important as a human being," he said. "We will never agree that we're going to violate law and regulation and not do certain tests that are required on animals. But we have agreed that we're going to be clear about where we disagree and we're going to respect each other's points of view."

"In fact we've actually engaged with them and we have built, I think, quite an enlightened facility up there at Iams. . . . I have to tell you those dogs at the Iams facility still live better than 99.9 percent of the dogs in the world." (PETA still begs to disagree; it operates a Web site called Iamscruelty.com, saying the animals are fed a "diet of loneliness, suffering and neglect in their laboratory cages.")

In Lafley's view, all this reflects a new view of the P&G consumer. "Here's the whole motivation," he said. "You are a consumer of Procter & Gamble brands and products, so I may have your attention for a few minutes a day when you think about purchasing them or using them. Then you are concerned about environmental issues. Then you are concerned about political issues. They might be concerns of your local village or community, or the global economy and the impact it's going to have on your job or your family's job or your brother's job. . . .

"We used to think we were just taking care of the consumer who purchases Tide and uses Tide." But now, "we're taking care of this whole consumer, who is also a citizen, is also a member of the community, has other interests and concerns. . . .

"We think about it as trust and relationship. We are a company of intangible assets. Our market cap is $200 billion, our fixed assets are $50 billion. So why is the market paying us $200 billion for what we could sell on eBay in a fire sale for 50? They are paying for our brands and they're paying for our people and their innovation and initiative. When you are a company of intangible assets, when you're a company that lives and dies on reputation and trust and integrity of your brands and your products, you've got to be credible with consumers."

It also reflects a different way of looking at the P&G supply chain. "The old P&G was vertically integrated," he said. "We used to own forest land. We owned pulp mills. We owned a lot of chemicals and manufacturing operations, and it was very vertically organized. Now we're very horizontally organized and, in fact, I would argue we're organized in these networks—these solar systems. And the suppliers are part of our community. Not just the direct suppliers, but the suppliers of the suppliers of the suppliers are part of our community. So we do have to think a lot more, when we do something, about the effects."

Lafley's views about corporate responsibility were forged, in part, during time he spent in Asia in the 1990s—including a stint in Kobe, Japan, during the earthquake there. "Our first concern was for our employees and their families and their safety," he said. "Second, we were concerned about our consumers. And third, our communities. Every weekend an amazing number of P&G workers went out into the communities."

That same approach informed P&G's actions when the tsunami hit Asia, killing, among others, a P&G manager in Thailand.

Like other CEOs I've talked to, Lafley said his adoption of what others call "corporate social responsibility" is in large part driven by employees. "Our employees want us to do this," he says.

The question, of course, is whether a CEO who has to tend to so many different interest groups, and worry about so many different concerns, can continue to focus on what the corporation does best: generate wealth for shareholders. "The shareholders hired the guy to be the CEO and not Procter & Gamble's representative to the world," said Steven Milloy, who runs a group called the Free Enterprise Action Fund dedicated to keeping CEOs focused on their responsibilities to shareholders . . . and away from responding to liberal activist groups.

But Lafley insists they aren't contradictory goals. "If we aren't successful, we don't have the right to do the other stuff," he said. "But I don't think it's a trade-off. I actually think it's mutually reinforcing. I think if you can be commercially successful and if you can grow sustainably then you have the capability. You can turn some of your capabilities to improving the lives more broadly of those you serve."

Which leaves the CEO with a lot on his plate.

"The responsibility is huge. That's the big change."

When the new millennium began, Bob Nardelli expected to be the next chairman and chief executive of General Electric—successor to the legendary Jack Welch.

He had worked hard for the job. He ran the company's power systems division, based in Schenectady, New York, and was generally acknowledged to be the best operating guy in a company brimming with talent. He had taken the power turbines business from $770 million in 1995 to $2.8 billion in 2000, and had its net income growing by a billion dollars a year.

Nardelli had already been selected by Welch as one of three candidates who had the potential to succeed him—the other two were Jim McNerney, who ran the aircraft engine business, and Jeff Immelt, who ran medical systems. Like the other two, Nardelli had done the necessary courting of the board of directors, playing golf with them every April at the Masters course in Augusta, Georgia, and again in July near the company's Fairfield headquarters.

On October 29, 2000, Welch made his decision. Immelt was the man he wanted to lead the company for the next decade, or more. He informed his board and, not surprisingly, they unanimously supported his pick. This was the old regime, before boards were willing to second-guess successful leaders.

Welch put off telling the three men of his decision until Thanksgiving weekend. At 5:30 p.m. that Friday, Welch called Immelt, where he was vacationing in South Carolina, told him he had "great news," and arranged for a jet to bring him and his family to Welch's house in Palm Beach. They spent Saturday celebrating and preparing for a Monday press conference. Then on Sunday, Welch boarded a GE jet in a rainstorm to visit, first, McNerney in Cincinnati, then Nardelli in Albany, to deliver the bad news.

Nardelli took the news hardest. Immelt was tall and smooth, a product of Dartmouth and Harvard, while Nardelli was shorter and rougher, a graduate of Western Illinois and Louisville universities. He knew that on the qualities that could be measured—operating results—he was the better candidate. So why was Welch turning to Immelt instead? He clearly resented the decision.

"Bob," Welch says he told him, "you're going to be an all-star CEO. There's a big lucky company out there waiting to get you."

It didn't take long. Ken Langone was a director of General Electric, and also deeply involved in Home Depot, the home building supplies store. The company had been founded in 1978 by Bernie Marcus and Arthur Blank, and from there grew like wildfire. Langone understood, however, that its spectacular growth had left it an organizational hash, lacking the central systems needed to keep such a sprawling empire running smoothly. The founders had made a mess of their creation. Nardelli was just the man to fix it.

On the Wednesday after Thanksgiving, Marcus flew to New York to meet with Nardelli. The next day, Nardelli met with the board's search committee. On Sunday, he met with the entire board. And Monday morning, he started his new job.

Nardelli threw himself into Home Depot with the same energy and enthusiasm that had characterized his work at GE. With military efficiency, he centralized systems, cut costs, and made order out of chaos. And his results were surprising. He cleaned up many of the company's problems, and racked up solid numbers. In six years' time, revenues doubled and earnings more than doubled. The company's return on invested capital averaged right around 20 percent. He opened 900 new stores and created 100,000 new jobs. He was, by his own estimate, and by his board's, doing a stellar job.

Nardelli spent most of those six years focused on fixing the business, and paid little attention to the big changes happening in the business world around him. "I probably got too focused on the idea that you do your job, you take care of your numbers, and the rest will take care of the company."

But there were three numbers that started to cause Nardelli trouble. The first was same-store sales—a measure favored by Wall Street analysts. As Nardelli opened more stores near existing stores, he began to cannibalize his own business—causing same-store sales growth to slow. Meantime, his competition—Lowe's—was starting from a smaller base, and was watching its same-store sales rise at a steady clip. Nardelli was more focused on overall revenues and profits; but the analysts kept looking at lagging same-store sales.

That, in turn, kept the stock price depressed. Home Depot's stock had traded for $68 a share at its peak at the end of 1999. But it was in the $40 range for the first months after he took over, and nothing Nardelli did—including an enormous stock buyback program—seemed to be able to put the stock on an upward trend.

The third and most troublesome number was his pay. In the final months of the competition for the top job, Welch had granted each of his three candidates a huge slug of stock options. That was in the heady days of the stock market boom, when profits and compensation were soaring. Moreover, Welch explained to his board they'd only have to make good on one set of options—the ones belonging to the next CEO. The other two men would quit before their options vested, and those options would become negotiating leverage for their next job.

He was right about that. Nardelli used his rich GE compensation package to get an even richer one at Home Depot. McNerney did the same at 3M and then Boeing. Within a few years, both Nardelli and McNerney were earning more money than the "winner" of Welch's contest, Jeff Immelt.

By 2005, Nardelli's giant pay package had attracted the attention of AFSCME's Rich Ferlauto, who put the company on his hit list. This list included other companies with high-priced executives like Bank of America, Countrywide Financial, Merrill Lynch and U.S. Bancorp. At each company, Ferlauto and his allies planned to offer a proxy initiative giving shareholders an advisory vote on executive pay.

Ferlauto used his contacts with the press to increase the pressure on Nardelli. He called my attention, for instance, to the fact that the Home Depot board had changed the metrics for one component of Nardelli's performance pay—tying it to earnings per share, a measure on which the company was doing well, instead of returns to shareholders, a measure on which it was doing poorly. It seemed a clear case of moving the goalposts so the CEO could score a touchdown.

Ferlauto's big victory, however, came on May 24, when the *New York Times* ran a front-page story by Julie Creswell detailing Nardelli's pay and perquisites. During his five years on the job, the story said, he had made a whopping $245 million. During the same period, his stock had slid 12 percent while archrival Lowe's had gone up 173 percent.

The story was somewhat exaggerated. It failed to point out, for instance, that $130 million or so of that compensation was in stock options that, at the existing share price, were completely underwater. But it had plenty of other details of compensation excess. It noted that Nardelli also got abundant perquisites, including use of a company plane for personal trips, a new Mercedes-Benz or similar car every three years, and a $10 million loan, which the company later agreed to pay taxes on. It pointed out, as well, that Langone had also headed the compensation committee that had paid New York Stock Exchange director Richard Grasso an astounding $140 million.

The story ran before Home Depot's annual meeting, quoted Ferlauto, and noted that AFSCME and other groups wanted to withhold votes for the reelection of directors, and also hoped to get a strong vote on their proxy measure regarding Nardelli's pay.

In response to the *Times* story, Nardelli made what he now concedes was a critical mistake. He told other directors to stay away from the annual meeting, and let him handle it alone. These shareholder meetings are a joke anyway, he thought, and would only provide Ferlauto and his allies an opportunity to make a scene. So he adopted what he later called a different "format."

As columnist Joe Nocera reported in the *Times*, Mr. Nardelli appeared at the meeting with two aides, but none of his directors—an extraordinary occurrence for an event that is supposed to be the one opportunity for shareholders to meet with the directors who supposedly represent them. In the front of the meeting room, there were two large digital timers.

Mr. Nardelli informed those in attendance that questions "would be limited to one minute one person." Each time someone stepped to the microphone, the large clocks started ticking down the minutes. When Mr. Ferlauto stepped up to the microphone and asked where the directors were, Mr. Nardelli responded: "They aren't in attendance today."

■

Nardelli had made a terrible miscalculation. He had failed to understand how profoundly the world had changed. Maybe annual meetings were an archaic ritual; but they were an archaic ritual created for communication between the board and the company's shareholders. By trying to, in effect, eliminate that ritual, Nardelli had made himself the poster boy for an army of shareholder advocates.

Within 48 hours, Nardelli recognized he was in trouble. He was scolded by a number of friends and mentors, including Welch. He put aside his other work, and spent two weeks on an uncharacteristic "listening" tour. He visited with 25 of the company's largest shareholders, and heard their concerns. When he was done, he admitted that he had made a grave mistake. He went on television with CNBC's Maria Bartiromo and apologized repeatedly for the error.

Several months after the annual meeting fiasco, Nardelli met me for breakfast at the St. Regis Hotel in New York. It was clear he was a changed man—he had had a frightening collision with the new world of corporate power, and was trying to change his ways as a result.

While struggling to deal with the new world, however, Nardelli shared many of Hank Greenberg's doubts about it. The forces that had attacked him, he feared, would also undercut the economic interests of the country. He felt the media was not giving him a fair shake, and that groups like AFSCME were being given too much influence.

"I am very concerned with the future of business and the capitalistic system in this country," he said. "Somebody has yelled fire in the auditorium. . . . If you stand back," he said, "you've got to say that we as a country should share a growing concern as it relates to the capitalist system. The things that got us to where we are are under attack."

One result, he noted, was the rush of money and talent into private equity. "But not everyone can go private. As everybody rushes to private equity, what happens?"

Most of all, though, Nardelli sounded like a man who had been shocked by the rapid change in the world in which he operated.

"I used to play football," he said. "In football, you always knew the score. Now it's like we are ice-skating, and you've got a bunch of judges on the sidelines shouting out scores."

But the one thing Nardelli refused to apologize for was his pay package. It had been given to him by the board, largely spelled out in the contract he had negotiated upon leaving GE. He deserved it, he thought, and no one was going to take it away from him.

I suggested it might make sense for him to announce to shareholders a voluntary suspension of pay. He could say that he was not going to accept another penny until he got the stock price moving upward again. If he succeeded, he would still be richly rewarded, since his options would rise in value. And it would show the shareholders that his interests and theirs were identical.

Nardelli responded with a smile, but said nothing.

In the months that followed, I later learned, Nardelli had similar discussions with his own board of directors. For the most part, the directors were supportive of him. Ken Langone even made phone calls to reporters, vigorously defending his pay and his performance. Langone was already a controversial figure in the debate over executive pay, having approved and vigorously defended the nearly $200 million pay package that went to ex–New York Stock Exchange chief Dick Grasso. His role in that affair had prompted New York attorney general Eliot Spitzer to charge him, in a civil suit, with misleading other stock exchange directors. Langone adamantly fought the charges, and was equally adamant in defending Nardelli.

But the board, and even Langone, realized that they had a serious problem on their hands, if only in terms of public relations. They asked Nardelli to consider tempering his pay package. Nardelli agreed to give up his guarantee of a minimum $3 million bonus each year, but no more.

During the fall of 2006, Nardelli and the Home Depot board had serious discussions about taking the company private as a way of avoiding public pressures. But in the end, they agreed that was not a good idea. Home Depot was too big, and it would have to take on too much debt to make a private-equity deal work. The idea was rejected.

Then on January 4, 2007, the company issued a press release. Nardelli and his board had "mutually agreed" that he would resign, effective January 2. He would leave with the compensation, valued at some $210 million, that was due to him. But he would give up the one thing he had always wanted in his career—the CEO's job.

CONCLUSION

There is probably no one who has thought longer or harder about the problem of governing large public corporations than Ira Millstein. He is a lawyer who began his career in the 1950s working in the antitrust division of the U.S. Department of Justice prosecuting companies, then went on to defend those companies as a partner for five decades at the firm of Weil, Gotshal & Manges in New York.

Millstein's work in antitrust gave him a clear sense of the limits of government as a check on corporate power. All too often, government prosecutors and regulators had become pawns in the competitive struggle between companies, rather than protectors of the public interest. Academic studies showed that antitrust enforcement frequently hurt consumers, rather than helping them. Likewise, government regulation of industry—be it airlines, trucking or telecommunication—created cartel-like structures that thwarted competition and propped up prices. By the 1970s, it was clear that government efforts to rein in corporate power had been, more often than not, counterproductive.

But if the government wasn't going to hold corporations accountable, who was? That's the question Millstein began to ponder in the 1970s, as a new era of deregulation, privatization and faith in markets began to take hold. Big public corporations needed to be held to account, he believed. But they should be held to account by their shareholders, acting through boards of directors.

By 1981, Millstein had written his first book on the subject—*The Limits of Corporate Power*. And by 1983, he was lecturing at the Yale School of Management and Harvard's Kennedy School of Government. For two and a half decades, he has been recognized as the nation's preeminent expert on matters of "corporate governance."

In the fall of 2006, I went to visit Millstein to talk about how the corporate world was changing, and the implications of that change. He works from a corner office on the 32nd floor of a building on Fifth Avenue in New York City, with windows offering a panoramic view of Central Park. "That's *my* park," he says, in a reference to his service as chairman of the Central Park Conservancy, but also to his status as a lifelong New Yorker, who grew up playing in the park.

Millstein understands how much the world has changed. "There has been a huge leap forward," he says. "I see boards as much more proactive than they were before."

When he first started representing boards in the 1970s and early 1980s, they were "very staid," he says. "The CEO really owned the boardroom. No question."

At the urging of Millstein and others, that started to change in the 1990s. The firing of General Motors chief executive Robert Stempel—which, as an adviser to the GM board, Millstein was a critical part of—started to change things. But the real catalyst came from the corporate scandals of 2002. In the aftermath, says Millstein "the *shoulds* became *musts*," as the government, the New York Stock Exchange, the public pension funds, and others began insisting that boards of directors adopt the kinds of corporate governance measures that Millstein had long advocated.

The most important of those changes, Millstein argues, was one of the simplest—requiring independent directors to meet regularly in executive session, without the CEO present. He had learned working with General Motors chairman John Smale in the early 1990s how difficult it was to have honest conversations at board meetings.

"John and I quickly learned that members of the board couldn't talk to each other," he told me. "They couldn't because the CEO was always in the room. Most of the real conversations took place in the men's room or in restaurants."

I asked Millstein whether the changes that had taken place in corporate power over the last few years had gone too far, or not far enough. Not surprisingly, his answer suggested some of both.

What has gone too far, he said, are some of the explicit requirements that Congress placed on boards as part of the Sarbanes-Oxley corporate reform law. The most egregious example, he said, is section 404, which requires companies to do detailed and costly audits of their internal controls. Millstein says 404 went "way too far." More generally, he said, the danger with placing explicit government requirements on boards is that they spend all of their time fulfilling those requirements. Instead, boards should spend *most* of their time, not on such compliance measures, but discussing the corporation's strategy, evaluating risks to the company, and monitoring its performance.

What hasn't gone far enough, he says, is the effort to make sure directors recognize they work for shareholders, not for management. This, in his view, is the major unfinished business of corporate reform.

The day I visited his office happened to be just one week after the Second Circuit Court of Appeals struck down an SEC decision that prevented Rich Ferlauto and AFSCME from offering an amendment to AIG's bylaws to change the way directors are elected. That ruling, Millstein argued, could hold the seeds of the next revolution in corporate power. Directors had become more powerful, but shareholders still had relatively little ability to nominate their own directors. The court decision could change that, making it increasingly possible for large shareholders to offer their own candidates for directors' jobs.

I reminded Millstein that many CEOs fear that change. Their arguments are twofold. First, they worry that activists will use increased access to the boardroom to push narrow agendas, like curbing global warming or boosting health care benefits. Second, they fear that allowing shareholders to offer their own director candidates will undermine the collegiality necessary for a successful board. The result of these changes, some fear, will be to make every board more like the Hewlett-Packard board—caldrons of dissent and argument that hurt companies, not help them.

Millstein had little sympathy for the first argument. Directors still won't get elected without majority support, he pointed out. So special interest groups can only prevail if they form broad coalitions, and offer candidates suitable to other shareholders.

The second argument, however, struck a chord with him. "I'm a firm believer in shareholders having the right to put people on the board," he said. "But I am also a firm believer in not having directors who you can't work with." Corporate boards should not become "a debating society." "You do not under any circumstances want the board to be like the U.S. Senate." There needs to be some sense of common purpose, and some ability to work together.

Still, Millstein believes giving shareholders more power to select directors can lead to the right result. Over time, he argues, boards will consult more fully with major shareholders before putting forward a slate of directors in the first place. "I like negotiated settlements better than fights," he says. "Giving shareholders power will frequently mean you don't have to use it. You'll have greater discussion between the shareholders and the board." Shareholders, he believes, will realize that a smoothly functioning board is important to ensuring that their investments are well managed. And directors will come to realize that they truly do serve the shareholders, not the CEO.

Giving more power to shareholders, however, raises another serious problem with the current structure of corporate power. Increasingly, mutual funds are the largest shareholders at most big companies. Yet mutual funds almost always vote with management—in part, critics believe, because they don't want to alienate companies that could throw business their way. A big mutual fund company like Fidelity, for instance, makes its money by running corporate retirement programs. If Fidelity's funds start voting against the directors chosen by management, or against the management position on proxies, the company risks losing business.

Indeed, that may be the biggest unfinished business of corporate reform. If mutual funds are going to own large corporations, they are going to have to take more responsibility for overseeing the management of those companies. If they refuse, Millstein's vision of corporate democracy is likely to fail. "You need shareholders who care," Millstein says.

Whether that ever happens, of course, depends in part on how long the public demand for corporate reform lasts in the years ahead. Will movement toward Millstein's goal continue, or will the progress fade as the scandals of Enron and WorldCom and Tyco fade into memory?

My own guess is that it will continue for some time to come—even after the names Ken Lay and Bernie Ebbers and Dennis Kozlowski become distant memories.

One big reason for that is continuing anger over CEO pay. CEO pay has become the one issue that, more than any other, is fueling a continued attack on the old regime. It's the favorite whipping boy not just of liberal activists and the press, but of average investors who see their stock holdings languish while chief executives pile up riches. Any of us who write about this topic quickly learn its power. Readers of all stripes and all ideologies respond with a flood of letters and e-mail, attacking the greed of corporate leaders. The rash of CEO dismissals has done little to tame their anger, especially when they see departing CEOs like Franklin Raines or Carly Fiorina or Hank McKinnell handed tens of millions or even hundreds of millions of dollars as they walk out the door.

Americans have always been unusually tolerant of wealth. The politics of envy has never had strong appeal for them. People are happy to see a Bill Gates or a Tiger Woods or a Katie Couric win huge riches because of their skills or their successes. In part, that's because Americans tend to believe some day they, too, could be the ones winning life's lottery.

CEO pay, however, looks too much like a rigged game. For years, pay levels were set with the help of compensation consultants, who were hired by management and thus had an inherent conflict of interest. Their standard modus operandi was to look at a rigged cross-section of comparable companies, and see what other executives were earning. Members of the board, convinced they had an above-average CEO, would provide above-average pay. The result was an ever-rising pay escalator. The stock market explosion of the 1990s accelerated that escalator, as executives with large batches of options saw their pay skyrocket, driving up average pay levels that then became the base of comparison for the next generation of executives. When the market collapsed, pay kept rising.

Under this system, public-company CEOs came to be paid like entrepreneurs, but with one big difference: they seemed to make millions even when they failed. It was a one-sided bet: heads, you win; tails you win even more. Stories by my colleagues at the *Wall Street Journal* about the widespread backdating of stock options in the 1990s reinforced the point. For too long, the CEO pay game had its own set of rules.

Perversely, the CEO turnover of the last few years has only worsened pay trends. As often as not, companies that ousted a CEO have felt compelled to look outside for his or her replacement. Wooing a CEO from another company has proven particularly expensive. Sought-after CEO candidates demand to be "made whole" for any options or other compensation they leave behind at their old employer, and want to be compensated for the uncertainty of leaving an environment they know to go to one they don't. That's how Bob Nardelli and James McNerney—the losers in Jack Welch's three-way competition to replace him as CEO of General Electric—ended up earning substantially more pay at other companies than the winner, Jeff Immelt, now makes at GE.

Moreover, CEOs have become symbols of compensation excess at a time when middle-class Americans have been losing out. Median wages have stagnated over the last two decades, even as wealth at the top has accumulated, testing Americans' traditional tolerance for an unequal distribution of riches. Concern about increased corporate outsourcing, disappearing pensions, declining corporate willingness to pay for ever-more-expensive health care, are all on the rise. Support for globalization, privatization and free markets, which characterized the last quarter of the 20th century, are being tested in the first years of the 21st. The attack on CEOs could be the leading edge of a much bigger and broader middle-class revolt that is only now rearing its head. If that develops, the attack on the old regime of the last few years could look tame in comparison with what's to come.

Are the sweeping changes in corporate power for the good? Will the new regime turn out to be better than the one that is being swept away? The reformers, convinced of the rightness of their own positions, are convinced that the answer is yes. They look at Enron, WorldCom, Adelphia and Tyco as proof that things had to change.

Some of the victims, on the other hand, like Hank Greenberg

and Bob Nardelli, are equally certain that the answer is no. They point to the chaos at Hewlett-Packard as what happens when diverse boards have too much freedom and power.

The CEO-centric corporation of the 20th century clearly had significant drawbacks. As companies like GM and IBM proved in the 1970s and 1980s, these huge organizations could become far too insular and impervious to necessary change. And as Enron and WorldCom demonstrated, CEOs on long leashes could, as Berle and Means had feared, run their companies to suit their own greed and ambition, at the expense of the shareholders who owned them.

Still, the old regime can also claim its successes. The United States, and to a certain extent the world, owes its prosperity in the 20th century to the remarkable success of the public corporation. It became the principal means for organizing high-value economic activity, and spreading it across the world. CEO-centered companies like Hank Greenberg's AIG, or Sandy Weill's Citigroup, or Jack Welch's General Electric or Bill Gates's Microsoft proved to be the institutional success stories of the century. Despite Berle and Means's misgivings, they grew and prospered and spread their benefits across society.

Any student of that history has to wonder whether something important is being lost in the current revolution. Hank Greenberg may be an angry refugee from an earlier era, but there's a ring of truth in his claim that he couldn't build a big public company like AIG in today's environment—at least, not in the way he did before. Jack Welch, the happy warrior who presided over General Electric during the last two decades of the 20th century, is less critical of current trends, but his charismatic and personality-centered style of leadership also seems anachronistic. These men had extraordinary freedom to run their companies the way they wished. No CEO in the foreseeable future is likely to have the same.

Academics have tried to settle this debate, looking for evidence that "good corporate governance"—i.e., an effective check on a CEO's power—leads to better performance for shareholders. So far, however, the evidence is mixed. In part, the problem is one of definitions. What is "good governance"? How do you measure "performance"? At the end of the day, the studies are inconclusive. The choice between the old regime and the emerging new one seems to be more a matter of faith and preference than one of reason or science.

NOTES

INTRODUCTION

Page

xi CEO departures: Challenger, Gray & Christmas, "960 CEO Exits Through August," press release, September 12, 2006.

xiii At times, he would poke Dunn . . . : Patricia Dunn, in an interview with the author. Confirmed by another director. Perkins declined to confirm or deny, saying, "I don't know what a clavicle is."

xiii Alan Murray, "Business: Director's Cut," *Wall Street Journal,* September 6, 2006, p. 1.

xix Gallup poll: The poll question read: "Please tell me how you would rate the honesty and ethical standards of people in these different fields." The poll combines "high" and "very high" responses. For comparison, car salesmen were at 8 percent, senators at 16, lawyers at 18, journalists at 28 and policemen at 61. Nurses topped the list at 82 percent. The poll was conducted on November 17–20, 2005.

CHAPTER ONE:
REVOLT IN THE BOARDROOM

1

3 "sell ice to Eskimos": Donald Peterson, in an interview with the author, January 2005.

3 the most powerful woman in business: Fiorina topped *Fortune* magazine's "Fifty Most Powerful Women in Business" from 1998 to 2003. In 2004, she was displaced by eBay CEO Meg Whitman.

5 Among Fortune 500 companies . . . : As of October 11, 2006, there were

10 women serving as chief executives of Fortune 500 companies. But this is a constantly changing number.

5 "You will never do that to me again": Carly Fiorina, *Tough Choices: A Memoir* (Portfolio, 2006), p. 39.

5 "until the lady leaves": Ibid., p. 30.

5 "Our balls are as big as anyone's in this room": Ibid., pp. 140–43.

5 highly unusual telephone conversations: This account of the directors' phone calls and their thinking in December 2004 and January 2005 is based on the author's interviews with three separate Hewlett-Packard directors.

2

8 Bermuda tax laws: Glenn R. Simpson and Ianthe Jeanne Dugan, "AIG's Murphy Had Key Duties," *Wall Street Journal*, March 29, 2005, p. C1.

8 never hesitated to call: SEC enforcement chief Stephen Cutler, in an interview with the author.

8 milking cows before dawn: For Greenberg's early history, see David Leonard, "Greenberg and Sons," *Fortune*, February 21, 2005, p. 104.

9 Snowball: The information in this paragraph comes from Monica Langley, "Palace Coup," *Wall Street Journal*, April 1, 2005, p. A1.

9 Jeffrey and Evan: See "Greenberg and Sons," *Fortune.*

11 One of the biggest benefits of being on the AIG board . . . : Monica Langley and Elizabeth Bernstein, "Greenberg Resigns from Two Nonprofits," *Wall Street Journal*, April 11, 2005, p. B1.

11 After the scandals at Enron and WorldCom . . . : Maurice Greenberg and Frank Zarb both talked about their relationship in interviews with the author.

13 "The cumulative effect of these measures . . .": Greenberg, speaking at *Chief Executive* magazine's CEO of the Year Award.

3

14 Then, the company's former chief financial officer . . . : Anne Marie Squeo and J. Lynn Lunsford, "Missed Connection: How Two Officials Got Caught by Pentagon's Revolving Door," *Wall Street Journal*, December 18, 2003, p. A1.

15 The son of a Tennessee coal miner . . . : J. Lynn Lunsford and Andy Pasztor, "Higher Plane: New Boss Struggles to Lift Boeing above Military Scandals," *Wall Street Journal*, July 14, 2004, p. A1.

15 "Maybe you didn't understand me": Ibid.

16 "You can rest assured that we will investigate every tip . . .": J. Lynn Lunsford, Andy Pasztor and Joanne S. Lublin, "Emergency Exit: Boeing's CEO Forced to Resign," *Wall Street Journal,* March 8, 2005, p. A1.

16 Leaving the committee meeting, Duberstein . . . : The account that follows is based on interviews by the author with directors of Boeing. Harry Stonecipher refused repeated requests to be interviewed for this book. When finally reached, Mr. Stonecipher said, "If I wanted to talk to you, I would have returned your phone calls."

17 John Reed affair: See Phillip L. Zweig, *Wriston: Walter Wriston, Citibank and the Rise and Fall of American Financial Supremacy* (Crown Publishers, 1996), Chapter 26. Also, Carol J. Loomis and Tim Carvell, "Citicorp: John Reed's Second Act," *Fortune,* April 29, 1996, pp. 88–98.

17 Jack Welch and Suzy Wetlaufer: See, for instance, "The End of the Office Affair?" *Economist,* March 12, 2005, p. 82.

18 Indeed, Stonecipher's predecessor, Phil Condit . . . : See "Boeing: What Really Happened," *BusinessWeek,* December 15, 2003, pp. 32–38.

18 "we passed on some things": Lewis Platt, in interview with the author, July 2005.

4

19 In their early days, companies were direct extensions of government: The next two pages rely heavily on the excellent book by John Micklethwait and Adrian Wooldridge, *The Company: A Short History of a Revolutionary Idea* (Modern Library, 2003).

22 But there was an inherent weakness . . . : Adolf A. Berle and Gardiner C. Means, *The Modern Corporation and Private Property* (Transaction Publishers, 1991).

22 "persons other than those who have ventured their own wealth": Ibid., p. 4.

23 "The separation of ownership from control . . .": Ibid., p. 7.

23 The economic power in the hands of the few persons . . . : Ibid., p. 46.

24 Kennedy was a financier . . . : "431 Days: Joseph P. Kennedy and the Creation of the SEC," at www.sechistorical.org.

25 No one symbolized the new age of corporate power more . . . : For more on Geneen, see Robert J. Schoenberg, *Geneen* (W. W. Norton, 1985). A more pointed account comes from Anthony Sampson, *The Sovereign State: Secret History of ITT* (Coronet, 1974).

25 A common joke at ITT . . . : Schoenberg, *Geneen,* p. 18.

25 His frequent meetings in Brussels were held on New York time . . . : Ibid., p. 123.

25 He once called a review session for the day before Thanksgiving . . . : Ibid., p. 198.

25 He did, of course, have a board of directors . . . : For an account of the McKinney affair, see ibid., pp. 156–58.

26 Even after the scandals . . . his rule continued unchecked: See ibid., Chapter 21.

26 "We have an economic system which . . .": John Kenneth Galbraith, *The New Industrial State* (Houghton Mifflin, 1971), p. 6.

28 Peter F. Drucker, *The Unseen Revolution* (Harper and Row, 1976).

5

34 The three people who called on Carly Fiorina . . . : The account of the January 10, 2005, meeting is largely based on the author's interviews with members of the board of directors.

35 Dunn's "opinions were frequently hard to discern": Fiorina, *Hard Choices*, p. 190.

35 Then there was George Keyworth . . . : Ibid., pp. 280–81.

36 two garbage trucks colliding: "A Talk with Scott McNealy," *BusinessWeek,* April 1, 2002, p. 66.

36 Former HP CEO Lewis Platt compared it to a bad game of blackjack: Lewis Platt, in an interview with the author, July 2005.

37 "We were an iron stomach board with Carly": Dunn, in an interview with the author.

37 as many as 130 speeches her final year in office . . . : Fiorina says this number is too high, and that all the speeches were business related.

38 "You've let H-P down . . .": Pui-Wing Tam, "Fallen Star: H-P's Board Ousts Fiorina as CEO," *Wall Street Journal,* February 10, 2005, p. A1.

39 The most powerful wake-up call for corporate boards . . . : Rebecca Smith and Jonathan Weill, "Ex-Enron Directors Reach Settlement," *Wall Street Journal,* February 10, 2004, p. C3.

40 At the meeting, Keyworth started arguing that Tom Perkins be brought back . . . : The account of this meeting is based on author's interviews with directors. Fiorina's words and Keyworth's in response are from *Hard Choices,* p. 283.

41 Perkins says he later called Fiorina directly . . . : Author's interview with Perkins.

42 It was that memo that Dunn held in her hands on January 10 . . . : Author's interviews with directors.

43 "There was no thought that Carly wouldn't continue . . .": Author's interview with Perkins.

43 "I don't think that managing a company is a board's job": Connie Guglielmo and Kathleen M. Howley, "Board Wanted to Run HP, Fiorina Says," *San Jose Mercury News,* October 8, 2005, p. 1.

44 The San Francisco board meeting began . . . : The account of the board meeting is based on interviews with directors.

6

47 Spitzer was investigating the insurance industry . . . : This account of Eliot Spitzer's investigation of Marsh & McLennan is based largely on the excellent book by Brooke A. Masters, *Spoiling for a Fight: The Rise of Eliot Spitzer* (Times Books, 2006), pp. 208–19.

51 "We are heirs to one of the most august . . .": Ibid., p. 7.

52 speech Steven Cutler of the SEC gave: Ibid., pp. 128–29.

7

54 Less than a week after . . . : The following account is based on the author's interviews with HP directors.

56 Directors of Hewlett-Packard Co., unhappy with the uneven performance . . . : Pui-Wing Tam, "Hewlett-Packard Considers a Reorganization," *Wall Street Journal,* January 25, 2005, p. A1.

57 I made it my mission . . . : Alan Murray, "When CEOs Have Tea with Tony Blair," *Wall Street Journal,* February 2, 2005, p. A2.

8

62 Frank Zarb was one person Hank Greenberg thought he could trust: The following account of AIG board deliberations is based on interviews with directors, including both Mr. Greenberg and Mr. Zarb, and others close to the situation.

67 Then on February 9 . . . : For contemporaneous press reports of the subpoenas, see Theo Francis and Jonathan Weill, "AIG Now Faces an SEC Probe over Its Books," *Wall Street Journal,* February 15, 2005, p. C1; and Ian Mcdonald, "Regulators Probe an AIG Pact with Gen Re," *Wall Street Journal,* February 18, 2005, p. B2.

70 The meeting dragged on for 10 hours: The best contemporaneous account of this meeting is in Monica Langley, "Palace Coup: After a 37-Year Reign at AIG, Chief's Last Tumultuous Days," *Wall Street Journal,* April 1, 2005, p. A1.

9

73 Harry Stonecipher met with his board of directors . . . : This account of the Boeing board meeting is based on interviews with directors.

76 Monday morning, the press release went out: For the best contemporaneous account of the events leading up to Stonecipher's resignation, see J. Lynn Lunsford, Andy Pasztor and Joann Lublin, "Emergency Exit: Boeing's CEO Forced to Resign," *Wall Street Journal,* March 8, 2005, p. A1.

10

77 Franklin Raines, an African American who rose from childhood poverty . . . : The best contemporaneous account of the troubles that led to Raines's demise is John D. McKinnon and James R. Hagert, "Damage Report: How Accounting Issue Crept Up on Fannie's Pugnacious Chief," *Wall Street Journal,* December 17, 2004.

79 Three months earlier, the most powerful executive in Hollywood . . . : Eisner's story is told in the excellent book by James B. Stewart, *Disney War* (Simon & Schuster, 2005).

80 Purcell had long been a controversial figure . . . : For the best contemporaneous account of Purcell's ouster, see Ann Davis and Randall Smith, "Delayed Reaction: At Morgan Stanley, Board Slowed Faced Its Purcell Problem," *Wall Street Journal,* August 5, 2005, p. A1.

83 Booz Allen Hamilton said 35 percent of North American CEOs . . . : Chuck Lucier, Paul Kocourek, and Rolf Habbel of Booz Allen Hamilton, "CEO Succession 2005: The Crest of the Wave," *Strategy + Business,* Summer 2006.

CHAPTER TWO:
THE BATTLE FOR THE CORPORATION

1

88 As an example, they cited the American Telephone and Telegraph Company . . . : Berle and Means, *Modern Corporation,* pp. 4–5.

88 "the separation of ownership from control . . ." Ibid., p. 7.

88 "comparable to the concentration of religious power . . ." Ibid., p. 309.

2

90 It took a crusader, Lewis Gilbert . . . : The account of Lewis Gilbert and Wilma Soss on these pages comes largely from a paper by Richard Marens of California State University entitled *Inventing Corporate Governance: The*

Emergence of Shareholder Activism in the Nineteen-Forties. An abbreviated version of the paper was published in the Academy of Management Proceedings 2002.

91 "It may be an unusual thought . . .": John M. Lee, "U.S. Steel Swayed by Persistence of Wilma Soss," *New York Times,* March 18, 1964, p. 57.

92 "to mourn attempts to kill instead of promote passenger service": Mary Jean Bennett, "Reading for Business," *Wall Street Journal,* May 26, 1965, p. 16.

92 "Nazi" tactics: Richard Jerome, "Evelyn Y. Davis: For America's Most Dreaded Corporate Gadfly, Being Pushy, Loud and Abrasive Isn't Just Great Self-Promotion—It Pays," *People,* May 20, 1996, p. 69.

92 The AITU . . . bought shares of stock . . . : Marens paper.

93 On April 28 of that year . . . : Honeywell, Gulf Oil and Commonwealth Edison anecdotes come from Alexander Hammer, "Disruptions at Meetings Aid One Business: Security Police," *New York Times,* May 10, 1970, p. 140.

93 The big event was the 1970 annual meeting . . . : "GM Easily Turns Back the First Assault from Within by Liberal Reform Activists," *Wall Street Journal,* May 25, 1970, p. 4.

3

95 As a result, companies felt compelled to gradually . . . : Michael Jensen, "Dissident Stockholders Begin to Get Somewhere at Last," *New York Times,* May 17, 1977, p. 54.

96 The campaign to get companies to cut off South Africa . . . : Mitchell C. Lynch, "Proxy Plea: Holder Groups Press Issue of South Africa at Annual Meetings," *Wall Street Journal,* p. 1.

97 The prevailing view in the corporate community . . . : "Castle & Cooke Inc. Has Very Dim View of Activist Holders," *Wall Street Journal,* September 13, 1979, p. 35.

97 Most U.S. businesses in South Africa . . . : "Business in South Africa," *Wall Street Journal,* August 18, 1978, p. 8.

4

99 compared the payments to "ransom": "Firms Pay Richly to Get Shares Held by Potential Antagonist," *Wall Street Journal,* January 8, 1981.

100 In 1982, Icahn threatened to take over . . . : Paul Richter. "Icahn Takes Business in Stride," *Houston Chronicle,* June 9, 1985, p. 17.

101 "Corporate raiders, like Boone Pickens and Carl Icahn . . .": Kittrell made

his comments in a speech to the Oklahoma City Rotary Club on March 25, 1985. Reprinted in "Vital Speeches of the Day."

101 Felix Rohatyn, who had helped Harold Geneen . . . : David Vise, "Pace of High-Priced Corporate Mergers Seen Continuing," *Washington Post,* September 16, 1984.

101 The raiders, almost all men . . . : Leslie Wayne, "The Corporate Raiders," *New York Times,* July 18, 1982.

102 Attorney Martin Lipton, who was the favorite consigliere . . . : Martin Lipton, "Boards Must Resist," *New York Times,* August 9, 1981.

102 But raiders like Pickens dismissed . . . : T. Boone Pickens Jr., "Professions of a Short-Termer," *Harvard Business Review,* May–June 1986.

102 "The peak of that buyout trend . . .": The RJR story is taken entirely from Bryan Burrough and John Helyar, *Barbarians at the Gate: The Fall of RJR Nabisco,* HarperCollins, 1990.

105 "In the history of corporate governance . . .": Rob Norton, "Who Owns This Company Anyhow?" *Fortune,* July 29, 1991.

5

106 Peter Drucker chronicled . . . : Peter F. Drucker, *The Unseen Revolution,* Harper & Row, 1976.

107 "The economics of massive institutional ownership . . .": James P. Hawley, "Political Voice, Fiduciary Activism and Institutional Ownership of U.S. Corporations: The Role of Public and Noncorporate Pension Funds," *Sociological Perspectives* 38, no. 3 (Autumn 1995): 415–35.

107 Leading the charge was California treasurer . . . : Fred R. Bleakley, "Jesse Unruh, Treasurer for California, Has Been Instrumental," *New York Times,* February 10, 1985, p. 6.

108 The council's existence reflected a sea change . . . : Hawley, *Sociological Perspectives.*

108 "If these institutions start speaking . . .": "Jesse Unruh: The Guardian Angel on Wall Street," *California Journal,* 1985.

109 Another critical player in the rise . . . : Hilary Rosenberg, *A Traitor to His Class: Robert A. G. Monks and the Battle to Change Corporate America* (John Wiley & Sons, 1999).

110 In a 1979 letter to Derek Bok . . . : Ibid., pp. 64–65.

110 Monks laid down the essence of his philosophy": Ibid., p. 98.

111 Shareholder activist Nell Minow . . . : John A. Byrne, "Governance: CEOs Catch Up with Shareholder Activists," *BusinessWeek,* September 27, 1997.

6

112 Until 1992: The following account of the General Motors board revolt comes from the excellent book by my *Wall Street Journal* colleagues, Paul Ingrassia and Joseph B. White, *Comeback: The Fall and Rise of the American Automobile Industry* (Simon & Schuster, 1994), pp. 277–321.

114 On another occasion, Smith stormed up to Millstein's office . . . : Author's interview with Millstein.

115 The firing at American Express . . . : Susan Pulliam and Steven Lipin, "Some Major American Express Holders Voice Disappointment about Robinson," *Wall Street Journal,* January 29, 1994, p. A4.

7

120 In a press conference on March 14 . . . : The transcript of Thompson's March 14, 2002, press conference comes from Federal Document Clearing House, Inc.

CHAPTER THREE:
THE NEW ORDER

1

131 Pattie Dunn says she never asked . . . : Sections 1 through 3 of this chapter are based on the author's interviews with a number of the participants, some of whom asked that they not be quoted. In addition, these sections draw on the extensive documents provided to the House Energy and Commerce Investigations subcommittee. Jay Keyworth refused all interview requests, although he made his lawyer, Reginald Brown, available to answer some questions on his behalf.

131 In her book . . . : Fiorina, *Tough Choices,* p. 281.

2

142 "H-P built up information . . .": Pui-Wing Tam, "I Spy—A Reporter's Story: How H-P Kept Tabs on Me for a Year," *Wall Street Journal,* October 19, 2006, p. A1.

4

156 "Having a quality CEO . . .": Author's interview with Zarb.

156 "Philanthropic contributions . . .": Author's interview with Levitt.

157 Just how much AIG changed . . . : Transcript of the AIG board meeting obtained from Thompson Financial.
159 In an interview with . . . : Kimberley A. Strassel, "The Journal Interview with Hank Greenberg," *Wall Street Journal*, April 19, 2006, p. 14.

CHAPTER FOUR:
THE NEW POWER ELITE

2

166 Richard Ferlauto is not the sort of guy . . . : This section is based largely on the author's interviews with Richard Ferlauto.

3

171 Patrick McGurn is an unassuming man . . . : This section is based largely on the author's interviews with Patrick McGurn.

4

175 "Sister Pat" sits in an office . . . : This section is based largely on the author's interviews with Pat Wolf and Mark Regier.

5

179 Just one hedge fund alone—Steven Cohen's SAC Capital . . . : See Susan Pulliam, "Private Money, the New Financial Order," *Wall Street Journal*, September 16, 2006, p. A1.
180 In September 2005, William Ackman . . . : Alan Murray, "Business: Attack on McDonald's Heralds a New Order," *Wall Street Journal*, November 23, 2005, p. A2.
181 In 2006, Ackman participated in another hedge fund attack . . . : Alan Murray, "Business: Heinz Is Better Served with Peltz Outside of the Boardroom," *Wall Street Journal*, August 9, 2006, p. A2.
182 The boldest hedge fund attack of 2006 . . . : Alan Murray, "Business: Icahn Should Admit Defeat on Time Warner," *Wall Street Journal*, January 25, 2006, p. A2.

6

183 In November of 2004, a group . . . : Alan Murray, "Business: Scandals Leave Big Banks Vulnerable," *Wall Street Journal*, April 13, 2005, p. A2.

184 "It was a huge win . . .": Author's interview with Michael Brune.
188 Sharp is part of the American Family Association . . . : Alan Murray, "Business: Gay Flip-Flop Turns Microsoft into a Target," *Wall Street Journal*, May 11, 2005, p. A2.

7

189 When the Business Council held its meeting . . . : Alan Murray, "Business: Business Council Welcomes Buy-Out Kings," *Wall Street Journal*, May 3, 2006, p. A2.
190 As proof, CEOs pointed to the story of David Calhoun: Alan Murray, "Business: Corporate Star Bets on Private Equity, and There's a Story," *Wall Street Journal*, August 30, 2006, p. A2.

CHAPTER FIVE:
THE NEW CEO

1

197 Moreover, CEOs now find they are constantly campaigning . . . : Chuck Lucier, Paul Kocourek and Rolf Habbel of Booz Allen Hamilton, "CEO Succession 2005: The Crest of the Wave," *Strategy + Business*, Summer 2006.

4

207 On October 29, 2000, Welch made his decision: See Jack Welch, *Jack: Straight from the Gut* (Warner Business Books, 2001), pp. 407–29.
210 Ferlauto's big victory . . . : Julie Creswell, "With Links to Home Depot Board, Chief Saw Pay Soar as Stock Fell," *New York Times*, May 24, 2006.

ACKNOWLEDGMENTS

Hundreds of people have a hand in the making of a book like this, and I can't possibly thank them all by name here. (Some would prefer not to be thanked.) But let me start with where it started—Paul Steiger, who may well be the wisest and fairest man in journalism, and who was willing to take this prodigal son back after three years in the wilderness and give me an extraordinary opportunity.

Thanks also to the others at Dow Jones and the *Wall Street Journal* who played their part in my return—Karen House, Peter Kann, Gordon Crovitz, Rich Zannino, Dan Hertzberg, Marcus Brauchli, and Joanne Lipman. They are all part of the most remarkable institution in journalism today, distinguished not only by its dedication to fairness and accuracy and relevance, but also by the character of its culture and its people. Virtually without exception, my colleagues at the *Wall Street Journal* welcomed me back with open arms, and were unfailingly generous with help when I needed it, which was often. I owe them much, for their sharing of knowledge, guidance and friendship. Forgive me for not listing them all here. But they know who they are, and I thank them from the bottom of my heart.

My colleague Joann Lublin deserves special mention. In addition to her frequent help on my weekly column, she gave an early read to the manuscript, and her eagle editing eye spared me numerous unnecessary errors.

In the publishing business, my guide as always has been Robert

Barnett, who, despite his ministrations to Bill, Hillary, Barack, Carly, Alan Greenspan, Bob Woodward and virtually anyone else who matters in the world of public affairs, has always had time to help me when I needed it. Herb Schaffner at HarperBusiness got this project started, for which I am grateful. Marion Maneker saw it through to its completion, and provided invaluable advice and editing on the manuscript.

A special shout-out for Lauren Etter, who did the initial research that made this project possible. She is an extraordinary researcher and an extremely talented young journalist, and she will be a star in this business that will brighten all of us who have the good fortune to work with her.

My greatest debt of gratitude goes to the very long list of people who have provided my education in the topics covered in this book. Some are mentioned in the text and notes, others have been mentioned in my columns, but most get no mention at all. Cynics think prominent people talk to journalists in order to keep their names in the press. But I know better. Most of these people who helped me had a very different motivation—a genuine desire to educate, spread knowledge and improve the world. I know I have been a constant drain on the time of people who have none to spare. Yet they have been amazingly ready and willing and patient with me, knowing that there was nothing in it for them except the satisfaction of helping a journalist trying to do his job well.

This project and the move to New York have taken an enormous toll on my family—Lori, Lucyann, Amanda—who chose to uproot themselves from a life they loved and come with me on the journey. They make it all worthwhile, and I love them for it. By the way, it wasn't *all* sacrifice: the weekends in Vermont, when they enjoyed the snow while I wrote, couldn't have been too bad.

And finally, thanks to my mother, Catherine Murray, who got it all started, typing out my first newspaper 43 years ago, and keeping me honest ever since.

INDEX